He Promised Me Roses,

But

I Forgot They Have Thorns.

A Reluctant Immigrant Story

By

Rose Dudley

Copyright © 2021 Rose Dudley
All rights reserved. No part of this book may be used or reproduced by any means, graphic, electronic, or mechanical, including photocopying, recording, taping or by any information storage retrieval system without the written permission of the author except in the case of brief quotations embodied in critical articles and reviews.

Books may be ordered through Amazon.

ISBN-9798484408467

Cover Design by Jennifer Givner, Acapella Book Cover Design
Formatting by Amanda Wyatt, awyatt199@gmail.com

DEDICATION

To all reluctant immigrants who have left a piece of their heart in their country of birth.

We look before and after, and pine for what is not.

Our sincerest laughter with some pain is fraught,

Our sweetest songs are those that tell of saddest thought.

— Percy Bysshe Shelley, *To a Skylark*

He Promised Me Roses,
But
I Forgot They Have Thorns.

PROLOGUE

> *The Pity Train has just derailed at the corner of Suck It Up And Move On and crashed into We All Have Problems, before coming to a stop at Get The Hell Over It.*

THAT WAS NOT BUT could easily have been written by one of those three husbands sitting across from us on the Sunshine Coast Ferry, in full agreement that they are sick to death of our whining, having put up with it for more than half a century.

My good friends, Chris and Tish, and I are lounging on the top deck, well into the topic that never fails to annoy the men, while enjoying the warm fall sunshine and gazing at the stunning views of the islands and the distant splashes of red vine-maple amongst the evergreens on the mountains across Howe Sound—Atl'ka7tsem. In another month, the iconic twin Lions, visible from many points around Vancouver, will be snow-capped enhancing what, we have to agree, is one of the most beautiful places in the world.

Many people are unaware that "The Lions" were originally named "The Sisters," [ch'ich'iyuy Elywikn.']. Legend relates that the twin daughters of a powerful Indigenous Chief persuaded him to make peace with a warring tribe, and the twins were made immortal through these majestic, natural monuments. The families that made the Peace Treaty and intermarried still live on the Squamish and Haida Nations unceded territory.

When the arrogant British arrived, however, they changed the name to "The Lions" because they reminded them of Landseer's Lions in Trafalgar Square. Of course, the First Nations' Elders were not consulted.

West Lion in winter—1654m. 5427ft.

The ferry plies its way across Howe Sound—named after Lord Howe, also known as Black Dick, which suggests that he may have been suffering from a rather nasty condition. He had defeated the French fleet in a battle that became known as "The Glorious First of June," during the Napoleonic Wars. Shortly, we will be able to discern a few scattered homes amongst the trees composing the tiny village of Lions Bay, along the Sea to Sky Highway to Squamish and Whistler, where I have lived for the past 49 years.

I stand up and stretch to breathe it all in and scan the water in the hope of seeing one of those pods of orcas or dolphins which have returned in recent years. Industrialisation in the past had polluted these waters to the point of elimination of much of the sea-life, but successful lobbying resulted in an expensive clean-up of the old copper mine at Britannia Beach and the closure of the pulp mill at Woodfibre. I try not to darken a perfect day by dwelling on the absurd government plan to reintroduce industrialisation which will largely benefit multinational companies which plunder the earth for profit—a plan that has turned me from that "Sloppy, Spineless Creature" of my youth into a sign-wielding, raging granny.

Raging Granny strikes again! Christy Clark was B.C.'s Premier at the time.

I sit down again, and we return to the conversation. Did we really manage to get through two whole days at the Davis's cabin without once bringing it up? We had laughed a lot, particularly about the stew that John had flavoured with trailing lobelia, being unable to distinguish it from thyme. We had covered all our favourite subjects—books read, politics endured, movies recently enjoyed, new aches and pains, upcoming tests and operations, rapidly approaching death and friends already dead, annoying in-laws, and grandchildren who were a "whole lot different in our day." Religion was no longer the hot topic that it had been in our student days. Other than one of our number—a good, practising Catholic upon whom we are depending to put in a good word for us if we are forgiven and find ourselves at the Pearly Gates—a supernatural being doesn't exactly play an integral part in our lives.

Our husbands, now leaning over the rail, do not look back, but we can guess that they are rolling their eyes in unison as we women compete yet again for which of us got the worst deal. They liken us to the four Yorkshire men in the 1967 Monty Python sketch, who try to outdo each other with stories of their deprivation. They know, as we realise, that we enjoy a lifestyle that is superior to that experienced in our homelands. My husband, John, never ever ceases to remind me and all our friends that having four bathrooms with indoor toilets that flush would seem to be a somewhat better option than the brick outhouse down the garden and the tin bath hanging on the outside of the house with which I grew up in rural South Wales. He brings it up again while the other John, John G, sniffs the air superciliously, telling him that he is sure that Chris would just love to go back to that refurbished Nissan hut in which she lived after the war rather than suffer here in her comfortable West Vancouver home. Basil chimes in. "Yes, I feel so sorry that we "dragged them to this cultural wasteland," as they are so fond of telling us, when I believe that Tish would genuinely enjoy sleeping with a gun under her pillow in South Africa."

The sarcasm emanating from the mouths of those men can be cut with a knife, but as usual, we end up laughing heartily together, knowing just how absurd the banter sounds and how many times we have had the same conversation. After forty or more years, it has become mainly tongue-in-cheek designed expressly to irritate the men. At this stage, all three women are very aware that they have enjoyed successful and comfortable lives in Canada, but even now they are not about to admit it, and in truth, they would all agree that the scars of those first years have not entirely faded. Speaking for myself, a few extra, hard to disguise blemishes have been accumulated along the way.

We had all arrived in Canada around the same time, being brought by husbands who had made the decision to emigrate. In my case, I had told John that I would follow him anywhere in the world. Love often causes the young and naïve to make hasty promises.

Those were the days when, as the proverb says, "As you must make your bed, so you must lie on it."

In other words, once married we did not think we had a choice. We stuck it out—grinned and bore it—regardless of how miserable life was.

Of course, that was a different time—when women tended to be more submissive, and before Germaine Greer—one of the major voices of the Feminist Movement—burst onto the scene. She explained Women's Liberation as a struggle for women to "define their own values, order their own priorities and decide their own fate." I don't think her views, however, would have made much difference in my case. They were far too radical for a "Sloppy, Spineless Creature," and when Gloria Steinem came on the scene a little later, I remember being somewhat critical of the Feminist Movement which seemed to be vilifying all men.

We know, however, that none of our daughters would have put up with what we had to endure in the early days. We tend to believe that we are made of sterner stuff.

But men, in general, do not understand and are not tied emotionally to their roots as are women, Obviously, and to our detriment, our men all belong to the "in general" category. They have no understanding that life is not about fancy homes with indoor flushing toilets; it is about being torn away from the very essence of one's beginnings, no matter how humble or disadvantaged those beginnings may have been. As Lemony Snicket—a.k.a. Daniel Handler, once said, "After you leave home, you may find yourself feeling homesick even if you have a new home that has nicer wallpaper and a more efficient dishwasher than the home in which you grew up."

We friends did not know each other at that time. We were all going through our reported "torture" separately. I often wonder if things might have turned out differently, if we had met and shared our discontent in those days and somehow, together, encouraged each other to believe that we did have a choice. We "suffered" in different ways, but the verdict is still out on who got the rawest deal.

Is it disturbing to be plucked away from a successful career, a close, loving family and a large circle of friends who one has no desire to leave to be cast into a strange land where you know no one? Is it worse to sacrifice your own career and be forced to move ten or more times in four years yo-yoing across the Atlantic along with your not-so-worldly goods and an increasing number of toddlers, while your husband tries to decide on which side of the ocean he wishes to practise medicine?

Naturally, I maintain that those scenarios pale by comparison to my situation. You may think it was a relief for me to escape from my crazy, knife-wielding grandmother, my dysfunctional family and the degradation of the British class system. I was, however, pregnant—though not entirely barefoot—on arrival, I knew not a living soul and was left alone for weeks at a time while my husband joined a tugboat as a deckhand. In retrospect, it was not exactly pleasant for him either. Every time he left me alone, I remember saying to him, "At least you are going somewhere." Well, he was—to suffer debilitating seasickness as he plied the coastal waters of B.C.—one giant step down from his officer days on a passenger liner. "My!" we said, "How the mighty have fallen!" I cannot refrain, however, from stating that the choice was his and his alone, and that I have never fully been able to come to terms with that choice.

But, fifty or more years on, despite everything, we seem to have survived our marriages and our lives as well or perhaps better than the average person, and so in the pages that follow, I relate a somewhat, but not entirely sorrowful tale.

CHAPTER ONE

When one door closes, another opens, but we often look so long and so regretfully upon the closed door that we do not see the one which has opened for us.

— Alexander Graham Bell

FIFTY-THREE YEARS AGO, Vancouver was not the beautiful and vibrant city that it is today. In fact, on first impressions, I was mystified why my husband had been so anxious to leave Henley-on-Thames—a picturesque English town set in bucolic surroundings—to emigrate to what was then such a soulless city that seemed to be cemented in the fifties. He likes to tell everyone that he was drawn to the closeness of the ocean and the wilderness, but I know it was the appeal of a career that promised him one and a half days off for every day he worked, although he obviously had not bargained for how unappealing that work would be.

Thankfully, when we arrived at Vancouver Airport, there was an absence of "Howdy Pardner" signs like the one that had alarmed me on our stop in Calgary. Perhaps we had not immigrated to the "Wild West" after all.

We were met by one of John's friends, Peter, with whom he had sailed in England—one of the merchant seamen who Lady Astor had called the "scum of the earth" when one of her daughters had picked up a nasty disease from one of those "low-lifes." Peter was, in fact, a soft-spoken, cultured English gentleman. He was the person who had tempted John with the idea of working as little as possible which appealed to him enormously.

Peter and his wife, Jacquie, had kindly offered to put us up in their Richmond home until we could get settled. Jacquie was the kind of woman who is described as "terribly English" with a plum-in-the-mouth accent which I, having been disparaged by the English class system, still found rather intimidating. She and Peter had two small children who John found rather more intimidating, dreading that shortly he was to have one of his own. He was still a rather immature twenty-four-year-old who just weeks before had been knocking back pints at the local pub, whilst singing bawdy rugby songs with his unattached former school buddies. Their principal objectives in life were getting drunk and chatting up "birds," believing they had what it took to entice them into the sack—pitiful, when you think about it.

He had always claimed that he did not want children. He once told me, soon after our meeting in Spain, that he preferred goldfish because when you were tired of them you could flush them down the toilet. But he had also told me that he did not want to get married until he was at least thirty, so things were not going quite according to plan for him at that stage of the game. He had tried to persuade me to accompany him to Canada without getting married, but even my naivety had its limits. I knew he was reticent about being married at such an early age, but if he believed he could be free to look for other fish in the sea if things didn't pan out, he would have found himself up the creek without a paddle.

We were completely in awe of Peter and Jacquie's home. The living area seemed enormous to us after our poky little English houses. It was open plan which was quite a novelty. The kitchen was huge with a fridge the size of an English garage and the living room had one of those fake teak feature walls which seemed the height of opulence to us. We did not know that almost every house had a fake teak feature wall in the sixties as well as a rec' room with a fake marble-topped bar. This house was a rancher, though, so we would not learn about fake marble-topped bars for a while.

After such a long tiring journey, I felt completely numb and unwilling to contemplate the immensity of what we had undertaken. John and Peter had lots to catch up on while Jacquie and I got to know each other. There were a number of other British ex-naval types living in Vancouver with their wives who we would eventually get to know. It was probably a good thing that I was not told that evening about one wife, whose husband had also sailed with John, who had drowned herself in Lynn Creek soon after being brought to Vancouver.

Jacquie seemed incredibly happy with the life she and Peter had made for themselves and was exceedingly scathing about the country that she had left behind. I wondered if I would ever reach that stage. On day one, it seemed unlikely.

We went to bed exhausted and fell asleep immediately only to be woken by something large and heavy leaping onto our bed. Reaching out my hand, I encountered warm fur. We had been warned, mostly by my mother-in-law, in a last-ditch effort to deter us from leaving England, that there were dangerous animals—bears, cougars, coyotes and raccoons in Canada, but it was dark, so we had no idea which of those terrifying beasts was about to maul us on the first night. Then there was a resounding thump as whatever it was leapt onto the floor. We lay there in fear, too tired to investigate or switch on the light, but then it leapt onto the window ledge and was gone. That ruled out bear, cougar and coyote. It would not be until the next morning that we learned that it was just the family cat, Telly, thwarting my legitimate excuse to return immediately to England to inform my mother-in-law that we should have listened to her all along.

I had not remembered the cat's name so contacted Peter who replied, "The cat's name was Telly, named after a Brazilian singer who used to jump through the spare room window at night which was pretty impressive with only one fully functioning back leg." He then wrote again to confirm that it was the cat not the Brazilian singer who jumped through the window despite a compromised back leg. I had realized what Peter meant, but it conjured up an amusing picture of a very athletic, Brazilian singer.

The following day, we had to think of all the responsibilities that had to be dealt with straight away—finding our bank, looking for accommodation, buying some furniture and getting a doctor.

The first concern, though, was to inform the authorities that I was a health hazard because I had never been vaccinated against smallpox. At London Airport the previous day, I was being taken away to be vaccinated there and then, when a doctor at Customs warned the powers that be that vaccination would be dangerous during pregnancy, so after much haggling I had been allowed to board the aircraft on condition that we immediately informed the Canadian Health Authorities that I was a grave risk to the population. Perhaps they were thinking back to the time when European settlers had devastated Indigenous populations by infecting them with smallpox and other diseases. Now, it seemed they were determined to protect their own descendants.

My husband was still getting used to the idea that I was pregnant, and he became very flustered on the phone. He blurted out, "I'm phoning to tell you that my wife is ten days pregnant."

"Well, congratulations, Sir, but I think you may have reached the wrong department," replied the voice on the other end of the phone, as we three doubled over with laughter. Now more flustered than ever, he tried again. "I'm phoning to tell you that my wife is ten months pregnant," he burst out.

"Really?" was the astonished response, "I don't think there is any way I can help you with this situation, Sir." More laughter.

Eventually, he got the message across that I was ten weeks pregnant, but no one really seemed to be too concerned that I had entered the country as a potential health risk.

Once that was settled, we thought we should deal with other pressing needs, but Jacquie decided that since we were so close to the United States, we should waste no time in going there. Without further ado, we jumped into her sporty Ford Mustang and headed for the border which she told us was only a 30-minute drive away. With her behind the wheel, we were there in less than 20 minutes with our hearts in our mouths as we tore through the Massey Tunnel at speeds that would make today's commuters green with envy. I turned green with fear as I saw death on my first day in a new country flashing before my eyes.

We were in Blaine before we knew it, but I do not remember being overwhelmed with excitement. Even today, Blaine is unlikely to evoke such a feeling, although the population has soared to 14,000 from 2,000 in those days, and there has been some effort to turn it from a logging and fishing seaport into an artsy-crafty centre.

I was already dreading the hairy ride back to Richmond, so I did not pay much attention to the impressive International Peace Arch which stands in Peace Arch State Park and was dedicated in 1921, symbolising lasting peace and amity between the United States and Canada. Lasting peace and amity were the last things on my mind. I was, however, standing on U.S. soil for the first time in my life, so it was something to write home about which I probably did that very afternoon.

The next day, we went in search of the branch of the Royal Bank that we had contacted through Barclays Bank in England. We had already been told that it was on Granville Street so, assuming that it would be central, we caught a bus and asked the driver if he could drop us off at Granville and Georgia. It was a blistering hot day with not a sign of rain, and we had been told that there had been none since April, but we had come from England where we were used to rapid changes in the weather, so we took along our faithful Pac-a-Macs.

Since neither of us had a working watch, John wrapped up the alarm clock in his Pac-a-Mac. The bus was crowded, and we had to stand. Suddenly, being still on British time, the alarm went off and everyone stared in our direction. This was long before terror attacks, so no one was freaked out as they would have been today. It took John what seemed an age to extricate the ringing clock from the Pac-a-Mac, and we thought if this had been on an English bus it would have caused some amusement, but as we laughed hysterically, our fellow passengers just stared at us in stony silence. We believed we looked similar to Canadians, but we obviously had "foreigner" written all over our faces.

As we hopped off the bus outside Hudson's Bay, we looked at the numbers on the buildings in confusion. They seemed to be missing a fourth number. We started walking south in the 600 block counting off the numbers and continued to walk across Granville Street Bridge realising the numbers would not increase until we reached the far side. Eventually, we arrived at our bank, 8585 Granville Street in Marpole, well over an hour later.

The heat was almost unbearable, but having dealt with the bank and realising that we were just a stone's throw from the North Arm of the Fraser River, we decided to carry on walking over the Oak Street Bridge, back to Jacquie and Peter's house on Fifth and Williams, not far from Steveston. We had walked a total distance of 20 km.

Well, that was day two, and on day three, already knackered, we caught the bus again in search of somewhere to live. Before we set out on our mission, we combed the streets for a different restaurant from the one where we had eaten the previous day—The White Lunch, on Hastings Street, which was part of a chain, the last one closing in the early eighties. We were made aware of the racism that existed in Vancouver in the early 1900s when we learned that it was given its name to indicate that the kitchen staff were all white. The patrons were also all white. Racism is still a major issue in our city, and sadly, has become more blatant during the pandemic.

There, we had ordered a tasteless bowl of soup and a white bun. Butter and a paper napkin came free which was a step up from England where one would have been charged extra. John remembers a sign in the window which said, "Where the Elite Meet to Eat." He assumed that Vancouver's elite expected white paper napkins as part of the service. Failing to find another option, we had to return for a second bowl of tasteless soup and a white bun, concluding that the elite in this city, at that time, were not too discerning.

All young immigrants in those days seemed to head straight for the West End. There were plenty of signs advertising appealing looking apartments for rent but none that accepted children. Forget dogs, cats and budgies—in those days, children were considered undesirable. Eventually, after another gruelling few hours of walking in the heat, we came upon the Beach Bay Towers at the foot of Davie Street which did accept children, and we were successful in renting a one-bedroom apartment there overlooking the pool and the beach for $140 per month, which seemed relatively inexpensive, but today would cost $1,650. Things were beginning to take shape, and as long as I kept my mind in neutral, I believed I might survive for the time being.

I said earlier that we did not know a soul when we arrived, but that was not strictly true. An old friend, Peter, from where I had grown up in Wales and who had once plied me with gin which he still chooses to deny, was living with a buddy, Winston, in the West End at Beach Towers. He had agreed to have a crate of our belongings sent to his address where we would eventually pick it up. We also knew that the grandson of my old vicar Phillips—the one who had terrified me with threats of hell and damnation throughout my Sunday School years in Wales—had recently married and moved to Vancouver and was also living in the West End with his new bride, Audrey. We would look them up as soon as we were settled, but before we moved into our new pad, we contacted Peter about our worldly goods—"our" goods being a misnomer.

Peter was exceedingly kind and decided to show us the sights of Vancouver and beyond. One day, he turned up driving an American car the length of which rivalled my old school bus. He took us to the Fraser Arms for a beer. If that was an experience aimed at persuading me that Vancouver had as much to offer as England, it failed miserably.

Peter was still a beer-drinking member of the single and carefree crowd to which John would have been trying desperately to pretend he still belonged. My only memory is of tables covered in sticky, red, beer-soaked felt which I found distasteful. I remember we had to be served beer at our table, and no one was allowed to move while drinking or carrying the beer. I believe this might have been in an effort to deter drunken loggers and miners—those who came back into town to squander their paychecks at the end of a shift—from getting involved in punch-ups.

I love British pubs for their atmosphere, but I have never been a beer drinker so could not relate to the complaints that cold beer did not compare very favourably to the warm beer that they were used to drinking in the "Old Country." Peter explained that the Canadian liquor laws were somewhat archaic. Fifty-four years on, I don't believe much has changed in that regard.

Now that we had acquired an apartment, we needed furniture. Jacquie suggested that we buy "A Three Room Group" from Belmont Furnishings which sounded like a good idea at the time. It included everything anyone would need in a home, down to cushions, cutlery, kitchen tools and glasses for the sum of $609.00 including tax. Hideous would be an understatement—think metal, vinyl and Formica—but this was going to be our first home, and to be able to acquire all we needed in one fell swoop, ready to be shipped to our new apartment, suited our needs. On August 1st, just eight days after our arrival in Canada, we moved with our cheap and nasty "Three Room Group" into our first marital home.

CHAPTER TWO

Choose a job that you love, and you will never have to work a day in your life.

— Confucius

SOMEWHERE ALONG THE WAY, reading those words, it would appear that I was not the only one who was naïve. John was about to focus on the last part of the advice, and I was going to take a job that seemed to be the only position available, other than becoming a prostitute, so choosing was not exactly an option. John was soon to discover that he might have done better to adhere to the advice of the person who said, "Don't pick a job with great vacation time. Pick one that doesn't need escaping from."

Now that we had a place to live in a pleasant part of town and we had spent most of our money on essentials, we both needed to find work. John thought that he would be easily hired by Island Tug and Barge, but I chose to put an advertisement in the paper because teachers in those days were not in short supply. My advertisement read, "anything considered." Some of the responses I received shocked me to the core and would be inappropriate to enlarge upon here, but it doesn't take a lot of imagination to be apprised. Slamming down the phone did not seem to deter the numerous creeps who offered me work.

Suffice it to say, that amongst the sexually explicit offerings, I did manage to land a temporary job as a filing clerk at Vancouver Volvo on Georgia Street for $200 per month.

Vancouver Volvo, I had always believed was the inception of the Jimmy Pattison Empire which would eventually turn him into the richest man in Vancouver and the fourth richest man in Canada, but I was wrong. The Docksteader family owned the dealership. I felt a bit let down when I discovered that. It could have been my claim to fame.

Within a week, I had completely organised the company filing system and asked for a raise. Two days later, they had found my replacement. Obviously, Don Docksteader, who would also become a multi-millionaire, was a bit hard up at the time. Fortunately, my advertisement eventually led to a teaching position at the Talmud Torah School on Oak Street beginning in September. The offered salary of $389.30 per month seemed like a small fortune compared with the equivalent of $195.00 that I had been earning before leaving England. Even at the exchange rate of $3.00 to the pound at that time, I felt we were about to be rich.

During my briefest career ever, at Vancouver Volvo—from August 11th until August 23rd—John still did not have a job, so he was able to make the most of the hot weather by sitting around the pool at the apartment, ensuring that the easy life he had enjoyed delivering paraffin in Henley-on-Thames stayed on the same trajectory.

Unfortunately for him, a position at Island Tug and Barge was soon to become a reality. There existed what appeared to be an impossible system to overcome at the time. To be hired, one had to sit in the Union Hall, but to sit in the Union Hall, one had to be a member of the union. The snag was that one could not join the union without having a job. For some reason, if you happened to be sitting there after 5 p.m. and a job suddenly became available, then it was yours, so that is how John managed to join the union and become a deck hand for the company. He was summoned to join the Sea Lion on August 24th, 1967. Having been hired and fired, I was now free to join him at the pool for just one day before his first trip to sea and until I started my teaching job on September 5th.

In England, his sea-going officer attire had been tailor made at Miller, Raynor and Haysom in London, but now he was about to slink unseen into Army and Navy on Hastings Street and grab some rough working gear off the rack. On his first shopping spree, he bought three heavy work shirts, one pair of jeans—his first ever—and three pairs of socks all for $13.60 including tax. At the same time, our records show that he bought an electric kettle for $9.09, surely the only thing that had not been included with the ghastly "Three Room Group."

I know that I have often moaned to Chris and Tish that I knew not a soul and was left alone for a month at a time while John was at sea, but I have discovered that he kept very detailed records of his comings and goings, and that first trip was only a week long. It was not until early November that he began to go away for longer periods.

In Vancouver in 1967, there was a rule that women could not teach beyond the fourth month of pregnancy. Was there fear that the sight of their pregnant teacher might warp the minds of small children? Was pregnancy considered too physically demanding? It seemed illogical to me. Anyway, I did not know if that same rule applied to private schools, so I thought it best not to broach the subject at my interview. Somehow, I believed that I could disguise the fact that I was only twenty weeks away from giving birth when I started the job.

The Vancouver Talmud Torah parents had high expectations of their children. I was hired to teach the English curriculum to a class of Grade Two students from 8.30 a.m. until 11 a.m. after which the students were taught in Hebrew until 2 p.m., and then I completed their day with the remainder of the English curriculum. They were bright and enthusiastic and seemed to cope amazingly well with the heavy load, and no one spoke of them being stressed out, a term which is used far too frequently these days.

Every day, I travelled by bus from the West End to the school on Oak Street. John had already gone to sea on my first day, so I had to figure out how to get there. I was already feeling alone and disconnected when I changed buses downtown so when the bus driver leapt out of his seat and came roaring up the aisle accusing me of not paying, I burst into tears with embarrassment. He turfed me off the bus while the stares from the other passengers pierced right through me like a knife and made me feel like a criminal. That was how I learned about transfer tickets. I could not help comparing this man's behaviour to the jocularity of British bus drivers. Years later, I know that such behaviour is not typical, but at the time I felt like sitting on the sidewalk and bawling my eyes out.

There was no genuine cause for me to be unhappy at the school—the children were delightful and the staff friendly and welcoming—but I was so conscious of my increasing size that I tried to hide it by keeping to myself.

The Six Day War, also known as the June War, had taken place between Arab States and Israel that year, making that the main topic of conversation in the staff room. Nasser had mobilised his Egyptian forces which had caused Israel to launch a pre-emptive strike. Israel had been victorious capturing the Sinai Peninsula, Gaza Strip, West Bank, Old Jerusalem and the Golan Heights, and the status of these territories subsequently would become the major point of contention in the Arab/Israeli conflict which has yet to be resolved. One older member of staff proudly wore a pendant of the head of Nasser around her neck, so I would not have dared to air my opinion on the subject for fear of starting another war. That was another reason why I kept to myself.

At the end of a long day, I dreaded going home to an empty apartment, seeing no one until the next day and having no way to contact John until he returned. But at least we were both gainfully employed in jobs that would keep the wolf from the door; John's first salary of $379.00 per month added to mine seemed like a small fortune at the time.

My only concern was wondering how I was going to announce to my headmaster that I was pregnant and would have to leave the school at Hanukkah. When the time came for me to leave, I felt sure that he and the staff had known all along, but they accepted my story that I had just discovered I was pregnant—I was just six weeks away from giving birth—and they wished me well.

John's concerns were clearly much greater than mine. As soon as he returned to the apartment after his first voyage, he began having nightmares. Our nights became much more colourful than the days. On one occasion, I awoke to find him in the clothes closet dressing and packing his bags to return to sea and in a panic because he could not find his silk tie to go with his Army and Navy work shirt. Another night, he was trying to tie a barge up to the bottom of the bed and directing the operation hollering "Hard a' starboard, hard a' starboard." Sometimes, he would grab me screaming, "What's behind this bed?" In a sweat, he would wake himself up explaining that he thought a chip scow [barge] was about to run us down. That must have been one of his greatest fears because on another occasion he had a nightmare that he was towing two chip scows down Georgia Street when the light suddenly changed to red. The job was taking its toll, and yet he evidently thought it was worth it to have all those days off.

Recently, when I asked him if back in those days he had ever thought that he had made a mistake, he was surprised by my question. "Never," he said with such conviction. I wonder what he would have said if I had posed the same question at the time. It is difficult for me to understand how he, uncomplaining, coped with that life at sea until 1974 when he was invited to take a desk job in the office. It wasn't until recently when our granddaughter, Amanda, he, and I were discussing jobs that we dreaded going to that he admitted that he had detested joining the tugs every time. I guess he was made of sterner stuff than Chris, Tish and I always believed we were.

He could write a book about his life on the tugs, going back to the day he joined the Sea Lion that had been built in 1904. Used to the formality of British ships and addressing the Captain as Sir, he stepped aboard the old tug and said, "Good evening Sir, I'm John Dudley, the new deckhand," and was surprised at the response,

"Hi John, call me Ron." This was Canada, so get used to the informality!

The Sea Lion was the tug that escorted the Komagata Maru that had arrived in Vancouver in May 1914 with 376 Indian passengers who were hoping to make Canada their home, out of the harbour. After two months on the ship, all but 24 of them were turned away by the racist government of the time.

I believe the dangers he faced while working on those tugs still give him nightmares. In freezing cold weather one January day, he was standing on the after-deck of a tug when a tightening towline flipped him overboard. As he went down, he found himself staring into the propeller, his lifejacket shooting him to the surface only seconds before he would have been sucked into it, but straight into the path of the 300-foot barge that was about to run him down. Luckily, a burly deckhand spotted him and hauled him back onto the deck of the barge in the nick of time. On another occasion, when it was dark and raining heavily, a tie-up line tightened and pulled him head first into the water where he was almost crushed between the dock and the barge which was being tied up. He just managed to save himself by clambering onto a boom between the dock and the barge.

I am grateful that he did not choose to divulge those stories until he was working behind an office desk. He was safely ashore when a tug went down in Howe Sound taking most of the crew to their deaths. My heart bled for all those wives, any one of whom could have been me.

CHAPTER THREE

First impressions are always unreliable.

— Franz Kafka

THERE IS NO DOUBT that Franz Kafka was correct, but my attitude, my condition, and my loneliness while John was at sea prevented me from seeing that Vancouver had much to offer.

We had arrived in a pivotal year—Canada had celebrated its 100th birthday on July 1st, 1967, and it would become a milestone year for entertainment. That birthday was the 100th anniversary of Confederation. The celebrations ignored the fact that the country had been populated by Indigenous peoples for tens of thousands of years.

Dan George, Chief of the Tsieil-Waututh Nation, whose reserve is located on Burrard Inlet in North Vancouver, moved a crowd of 30,000 people to silence with a poem, "Lament for Confederation." beginning, "How long have I known you, Oh Canada? A hundred years? Yes, a hundred years and many, many seelanum [lunar months] more. And today, when you celebrate your 100 years Oh Canada, I am sad for all the Indian people throughout the land."

As well as his writing and political activism, Chief Dan George had a distinguished acting career and was nominated for an Academy Award as best supporting actor playing opposite Dustin Hoffman in the 1970 movie, Little Big Man.

It is taking a long time for the European settlers to accept that they unlawfully stole the land from those who were already here, but when the 150th birthday rolled around in 2017, Indigenous people were invited to engage in debate as to how to represent their thousands of years of history within a celebration that had focussed on more recent history. The number of years in 2017, therefore, became 150+ recognising the legacy of thousands of years of First Nations culture.

It would take me years to become interested in or to understand the devastating role that our forefathers had played in their settlement of the country, but as a result of the Confederation celebrations we would learn that Vancouver was much more of a happening place than I was allowing myself to notice or in which I had the slightest interest in participating.

If we had been so inclined, we could have had a night out at one of the two hottest supper clubs in town—Isy's or the Cave—where one could have enjoyed a soft drink while secretively adding one's own choice of booze and listened to some of the well-known music icons of the day—Dusty Springfield, Chubby Checker, Little Richard, Duke Ellington, and Sammy Davis Junior. Failing that, we could have kicked up our heels on the spring dance floor at the Commodore Ballroom which, as I write, has just turned 90-years-old. Colin James, a well-known music star, and former Lions Bay resident, who is presently appearing there to celebrate the milestone year commented, "The Commodore brings out that stomp and keep-the-room-rocking thing," which is undoubtedly true, but fifty years ago stomping and rocking were the last things on the minds of an intermittently recovering sea-sick, tugboat deckhand and his newly married, pregnant wife.

It surprises me that we did not investigate the theatre and musical opportunities. We could have listened to Victor Borge or the New York Philharmonic Orchestra with Leonard Bernstein or watched the Royal Ballet with Rudolph Nureyev and Margot Fonteyn. We could have enjoyed a play at the Vancouver Playhouse—The Ecstasy of Rita Joe featured there in November—or seen The Odd Couple at the Arts Club Theatre. In England, we had been theatre and music buffs and often travelled to London for cultural stimulation, but here I was unaware that we had all those opportunities within walking distance. It would appear that Chris, Tish, and I were not actually "dragged to a cultural wasteland," as we would have our husbands believe, after all.

We felt we were well off but not quite enough to experience the fine dining at the William Tell, or Hy's at the Sands which was right across from our apartment block. By the time Frank Baker's had opened on the other side of the Lions Gate Bridge in West Vancouver, we had moved to Richmond. That was quite a funky establishment which we would frequent in later years. Women will remember that there was a statue of David with a cover over the penis, in the ladies' restroom. When a woman lifted the cloth, a loud siren would ring throughout the restaurant, causing much embarrassment to the lady as she returned to her seat.

I am not sure why we did not think of going out for dinner which we had done often enough in England. Perhaps, we failed to find affordable places other than The White Lunch, where we had ended up on our first trips into town, or maybe we recognised that by the end of the following year we would be able to afford to buy a house if we saved hard enough.

So, how did we fill our time? Our first priority was to collect our crate of belongings from Peter's apartment which was particularly exciting for my husband as it was mainly filled with his book and record collections. Knowing that we were planning to emigrate soon after we were married, he had decided that it would make sense to ask our wedding guests for cash rather than accept "heavy stuff that would be expensive to ship abroad." I agreed that we would save money that way until I realised that his whole collection of books and records, plus his typewriter, radio and sextant amounted to much heavier stuff. I had managed to squeeze in a pair of bathroom scales, a wedding gift from our cousin Pat, and a set of kitchen tools, both of which are still in use 54 years on. The scales, of course, weigh in stones so confuse our guests, many of whom are still struggling to convert pounds to kilograms. It is really not that difficult to calculate when you understand that a stone is the equivalent of 14 pounds and 2.2 pounds are equal to a kilogram. Wrapped around all of those items were an abundance of towels, nappies and baby clothes snuck in by my mother-in-law.

Now that we had a library of books, all of which we still own but realise will be tossed out as soon as we snuff it, we needed a bookshelf—another glaring omission from the "Three Room Group." The standard bookcase in those days consisted of a few lengths of board supported by cement blocks, so soon we had a make-shift bookcase to enhance the abominable vinyl, metal, and Formica. furniture. It was important to have lots of books on display, to demonstrate to those who might visit in the future that we were part of the British brain drain.

In John's records, I see that we had paid $5.40 to the Vancouver Sun in August. I cannot recall if that was for a monthly subscription or to pay for the infamous advertisement, the responses to which still give me the creeps. If it was for a subscription, then I should have been keeping up with news in the city and around the province, but I was still hankering after news of England.

I did not know, for instance, that the noise coming from atop the B.C. Hydro building was the first four notes of O Canada. I did not realise that the once famous annual Nanaimo bath-tub race had taken place only seven days after our arrival. I am surprised that I was not aware, at the time, that Greenpeace, now the largest environmental organisation in the world and of which we are avid supporters, had begun in a private home or a church basement in Dunbar under the name: "Don't Make a Wave."

There has always been some controversy over who the actual Founders of Greenpeace were, but there is no doubt that Paul Cote, Irving and Dorothy Stowe and Jim and Marie Bohlen were the Founders of "Don't Make a Wave" and that they were originally protesting the testing of hydrogen bombs at Amchitka in the Aleutian Islands. It is difficult for me to believe that I only learned of the Vancouver connection when we came across a group of protesters while cycling along the Danube with Chris and John G about twelve years ago.

They may not remember that incident because we were weaving our way along the trail after drinking copious amounts of liquor at the home of an Austrian gentleman who John G had befriended in a bar the previous evening. Gerhardt had told us that we would be cycling right past his home so insisted that we call in where, apart from getting us all tipsy, he regaled us with horror stories of his childhood.

He told us how he and his school friends had invented a competitive game which involved counting the number of SS troops shot by the Russian occupiers and left on the ground to rot every day. He shocked us with a story about the level of poverty that his family had endured throughout and after the war years—having no shoes, he followed cows in the fields in bitterly cold winters to warm his feet by burying them in still-steaming cow-pats. He was horrified by what had happened at the Mauthausen Concentration Camp just minutes away at the top of the hill, where over 90,000 innocent people had been murdered but claimed that his family and the neighbours knew nothing about it. I digress only to illustrate that one brief chance meeting can teach us more about our world in an hour than years of formal education.

More recently, we came upon a touching memorial to The Rainbow Warrior, a Greenpeace ship now an artificial reef in Matouri Bay, New Zealand. She had been protesting French nuclear testing when she was blown up in Auckland, killing one member of the crew.

Returning to the story of Vancouver in the 1960s, history buffs may be interested in a few other facts that I have since discovered but in which I had no interest at the time: 1967 was the year that the Vancouver Aquarium expanded to two killer whales, Skana and Hyak, the Blue Horizon was built on Robson, the roof was being installed on the Pacific Coliseum, the first issue of the Georgia Straight appeared in May at a cost of 10c, Nancy Green was pronounced Athlete of the Year, and the first McDonalds opened on No. 3 Road in Richmond

Memorial to "Rainbow Warrior", Matouri Bay, New Zealand

selling hamburgers for 18c. Television buffs may be interested to know that Pamela Anderson who has gained international recognition for her role as C J Parker in Baywatch, amongst other attributes, was Canada's Centennial baby, born on July 1st in Ladysmith on Vancouver Island.

One of the most interesting stories concerns the Jack Harman sculpture, "The Family," which graced the front of the Pacific Press building at 2250 Granville. We had missed it when we walked right past it with a mere 6,335 more blocks to go on day one. I do recall the controversy over the naked boy and the vandal who tried to saw off the penis. Apparently, the welder only agreed to repair the damage if he could do it without being seen, demonstrating that Vancouverites were rather prudish.

This is also illustrated by the fact that the Mayor at the time —Tom Campbell—also known as "Tom Terrific" had tried to ban the Georgia Straight and continued throughout his tenure to clash with the youth counterculture. I think everyone living in Vancouver in 1971 will remember the Gastown Riots where he ordered police on horseback to charge into a group of 1000 hippies having a "smoke-in."

More controversial, though, was his push for development—it was he who was responsible for the building of the first underground mall—Pacific Centre—and the construction of a huge hotel—the Bayshore Inn. Both of these initiatives were carried out with much opposition. It makes one think about the resistance to so many enterprises that eventually have been proven to be beneficial—the Sea Bus, Caulfield Shopping Centre and the Sea to Sky Highway to name a few. He was, for the most part, a forward-thinking Mayor. It may not have been a good idea of his, however, to have a freeway built through the East End, but considering the disgrace to the city which that area of Vancouver has become over the last 50 years, perhaps that may not have been such a bad plan either.

Not long after we had established ourselves and had begun to explore the West End and Stanley Park, we felt it was time to look at a list of addresses of people who our friends and acquaintances in England were convinced would be dying to see us as soon as we arrived in Canada. Several of those contacts lived in Nova Scotia, closer to England than we were now living. There were others in Quebec and Ontario, but one was an address just around the corner on Pendrell Street. I suggested that we should visit those people before becoming reacquainted with Michael Phillips and his wife.

One evening, we walked to the apartment on Pendrell Street and knocked on the door. The occupants looked quite mystified, and it was obvious that our mutual friend in England had not warned them that we might call. Nevertheless, Marie and Colin Moores welcomed us with open arms and over fifty years later we still consider them amongst our closest friends. It was also entirely through them, over the years, that we became connected to so many other close friends.

Like Peter, they kindly showed us around, taking us on outings outside the city. As Peter had done, they drove us up the Squamish Highway to admire the views of Howe Sound. We had no idea that in the future we would be enjoying that view every day from our home.

Mike & Audrey Phillips, many years later, visiting from Bargoed, Wales.

One memorable trip was to the Abbotsford Air Show on the hottest day I can ever remember. We have since heard that if you wish to choose a day with sunshine, you cannot go wrong if you pick the same day as the Abbotsford Air Show, and it seems to hold true. That day, I had to sit in John's shadow to find any shade. I was already three months pregnant and sick with the heat.

Together, we started going to the movies. There were some great ones showing that year, including Ulysses which was somewhat controversial. It had been banned in Ireland for being "subversive to public morality." In some countries, the dialogue that was considered offensive had been replaced with a variety of loud noises rendering it unintelligible. In New Zealand, it had been restricted to gender-segregated audiences, and I was in full agreement with that arrangement because when Molly Bloom uttered the word "fuck," I blushed scarlet in the dark, and when the lights went up at the end, I couldn't look Colin and Marie straight in the eye. Other classic movies we enjoyed that year were, Who's afraid of Virginia Woolf?, Born Free, A Man for All Seasons, and The Graduate, many of which we have watched again in recent years.

We had established a strong friendship with Colin and Marie by the time we walked around to visit Michael Phillips and his new bride, Audrey. I had not seen Michael since he and his brother, David, had participated in our wild games of Postman's Knock at Christmas parties in Tregaer Church Hall in Wales, but I recognised him instantly. He and his wife, Audrey, would also become life-long friends. So, from knowing no one on arrival, we had already made connections nearby and with other naval types further afield to whom Jacquie and Peter had introduced us. Things could have been worse.

CHAPTER FOUR

Everything happens for a reason. Sometimes the reason is that you're stupid and make bad decisions.

— Marion C Harmon

LET ME BE HONEST—our next decision did not happen for any reason other than we were just plain stupid. Yes, I had been lonely when John was at sea, but we had made friends with two British couples with whom we had much in common. They were within walking distance and were kind enough to look out for me in his absences. I was desperately lonely, but it was not entirely doom and gloom at that stage.

I believe we were not only the Founders of the "Could Have, Should Have" club, but became life-time members. Almost 50 years on, travelling with friends in India and Bhutan, we got ripped off at every turn, and each time we announced with conviction, "At least we've learned our lesson." Sadly, we never have. I am reminded of that every time I look at my ugly knock-off, "genuine" Indian rug, for which I paid much more than I would for the real thing available in Vancouver.

Looking back, I do not know why we thought we needed a two-bedroom apartment to accommodate another human being who would not be more than seven or eight pounds and 21 inches long. We were living in one of the few apartment blocks which accepted children so we could have carried on living there happily with the new baby, in a pleasant part of town.

Michael and Audrey were settled in an apartment on Broughton Street owned by a well-known character, Alex De Cimbriani, who lived at Erkindale Apartments in the West End. He had been carrying out classy renovations on old buildings there and called himself "The Mayor of a City Within a City." We approached him about an upcoming renovation that would be completed by November and paid a deposit. November came, but the renovation had not begun. We had already handed in our notice at our apartment so were obliged to move in.

If we thought the mighty had fallen to their lowest level, we were mistaken. The primitive home in which I had grown up in Wales was a palace compared to that place. We could not arrange our furniture because we were assured that the renovations were about to begin. We threw a mattress and some bedding on the floor and managed to unpack enough kitchen supplies to cover our immediate needs for the foreseeable future. The rest of our belongings remained stacked up against the wall or in boxes. We ate dinner out in a sleazy café that we had discovered, on days that Michael and Audrey could not invite us to eat with them. They were in no way responsible, but were feeling awful for unintentionally landing us in such a plight.

John was on leave for the first few days which made the situation somewhat bearable. Every morning, I did my best to make myself presentable enough to go to work without the convenience of heat, hot running water, a bathroom, or even a mirror. I boiled water in the kettle so that I could wash. I had grown up in such circumstances, but had not believed I would be reduced to living in such squalid conditions in "the country of opportunity." It wasn't exactly the beautiful home with roses climbing up the front porch that I had envisioned. My daily journey was, at least, facilitated by Michael who dropped me off at Talmud Torah on his way to the school where he taught in South Vancouver.

On about the fifth day after we had moved in, I walked up the street on my way home from school curious about the loud music emanating from the vicinity of our apartment. I recognised Gershwin's Rhapsody in Blue which was the very piece that John had played—reducing me to tears—every time he had gone away to sea in England. This could not be just a coincidence. Opening the door, I found him sitting on an unpacked box of books in our newly acquired hovel with the volume turned up to maximum and looking mighty pleased with himself.

Without consultation and with far too much free time on his hands, he had gone out to purchase a Zenith Circle of Sound stereo for $246.45—almost double our rent. He was so excited to demonstrate its features, moving the speakers around the dingy room to obtain the utmost in stereo effect that he could not understand why I was so pissed off. From then on, he would not be able to relax by the pool, but he could while away pleasant hours listening to his extensive collection of classical music while his pregnant wife was slaving away at school. My only satisfaction came from knowing that there was nowhere comfortable for him to sit and the musty smell might eventually drive him up the wall or with luck, choke him. A fleeting thought went through my mind that I could leave him there to rot and board the next plane home. That would have given Mr. De Cimbriani quite the shock when he eventually came to renovate the place.

Too soon, the day that I had been dreading came. By the time I got home from school, John had departed to join the Island Navigator and would not return for three weeks. I was left alone in a place that was unfit to live in.

Audrey insisted that I move in with her and Michael. I felt awkward about living with a newly married couple who just felt obligated to help me out. Besides that, when one is lonely, one often prefers to be alone to wallow in the depths of one's own misery. I knew I could not stay in our hovel by myself, however, so I reluctantly agreed. To allow them their privacy, I often told them that I had places to go just to get out of their way, but I had no place to go, so I spent many evenings wandering aimlessly around the West End feeling dejected and alone in the world.

By the time John returned, we had both realised that we had to move on. We had made one stupid move, but now we were about to make another one. We still believed we needed a two-bedroom apartment, but the only one available at such short notice was out on Joyce Road, in the Kingsway region. I remembered it as grey and depressing without a tree or a blade of grass 54 years ago, and a recent trip there with my granddaughter proved that time has done it no favours.

It was an hour-long bus ride to go to look at the place and meet the owner. He asked John what he did for a living to which John replied, "My wife's a teacher," believing that he would be judged, as one would be in Britain, for being a mere deckhand. I discovered while writing this memoir that he still has a bit of a hang-up about it. He balked at the idea of me choosing a title which described myself as a deckhand's wife. It's true that he was in that role for only a short time until he had become familiar with the B.C. coast. After that, he was promoted to Mate—which sounds more impressive than it actually was—and from then on, he was referred to as "Gentleman John" in the company, because of his educated British accent.

As it turned out, the landlord, Abe, had a son who was a student at Talmud Torah, so we were a shoo-in. The apartment was newly renovated and smelled of fresh paint, so we took it immediately, even though the area had nothing to recommend it, and it was miles away from the friends we had made.

Living so far away from them and with the new baby arriving in two months, we knew we would need transportation. John had bumped into an acquaintance from England in the West End, several weeks before, who had connections with dodgy car salesmen, so he called him, and he agreed to come to pick John up at our apartment.

My last words as they left were, "Remember, we only need a small car." Imagine my astonishment then, when only a few hours later they parked at the curb in an old beaten-up Pontiac Laurentian, one of the biggest cars on the road.

"It was such a good deal," they explained. Yes, it was such a good deal that when we attempted to drive over Second Narrows Bridge it could not make it up the slope to mid-point, although I have to admit it was superb on the downhill. We have no record of what it cost or if we took a loss when we turned it in three months later and bought a brand-new Vauxhall Viva—"We need a reliable British car," we said. That turned out to be a bit of a lemon so was our first and last British car.

Pontiac Laurentian – big enough to live in if we got desperate.

I only had three more weeks left before leaving Talmud Torah. By that stage, the news of my pregnancy was out in the open, so I felt more relaxed. The staff and the parents were so happy for me. I was sad to leave my little charges and the teachers I had befriended but relieved to be able to put my feet up for a while, spruce up our new apartment and prepare for the baby.

I purchased a 35-year-old Singer sewing machine from a store on Fraser Street, so that I could make curtains to replace the sheets on the windows facing the pavement. Now that my husband is going through his fanatical "save the world from consumerism" phase, he quotes daily from The Waste Makers written by Vance Packard in 1960 and proudly wears a sweater that his mother knitted for him 57 years ago. He also has many pairs of jeans inherited from a colleague with whom he worked 25 years ago which, depending on the season, he proudly calls, "The Wayne Biggars Summer Collection," or "The Wayne Biggars Winter Collection." That Wayne is about two inches shorter doesn't faze him in the slightest. I like to remind my husband that he doesn't need to lecture me—that I am on board with his passion, using a now 86-year-old sewing machine that is still capable of repairing his second-hand jeans, and weighing myself in stones on a 54-year-old set of bathroom scales.

Fortunately, John was on leave for Christmas that first year. Colin and Marie invited us to spend it with them along with some other stragglers who had no place to go. I only remember Dave and Kerry McPhedran being there along with a single girl, Judy, who worked with Marie and kept her on her toes by threatening to commit suicide every other week. I have no doubt that Judy is alive and well somewhere in the world and enjoying a productive life in her seventies. There may well have been two other English girls there, Linda and Anne, who had just arrived in the country. Anne had to leave after four months because she failed to have a bowel movement, but Linda, I assume, didn't suffer from the same condition because she met and married Dennis, a Scot, and they still live in West Vancouver.

I know we all had a jolly time, and we were so grateful to Marie and Colin for getting us through what could have been a depressing period by creating a family Christmas. In future years, we would spend many memorable Christmases with them along with huge numbers of stragglers at the home of other immigrants—Max, a German and Val, a Brit., who mean a lot to us. Those Christmas dinners at Max and Val's were legendary. They continued until the numbers of children and grandchildren became so unwieldy that they had to come to an end. I know there were around 36 of us at the last one.

"Auntie" Marie with Helen, Alexis and Daniel—Christmas 1971

Christmas dinner at Val and Max's—one of many. Note the ties!

We had met Max and Val at a dinner party hosted by Marie and Colin where Max remembers John amusing him, or perhaps shocking him, with stories of how bodies of people who died at sea on passenger liners were disposed of. I believe that was when Max decided that a cruise was not high on his bucket list.

And the underage drinkers getting sloshed at their own table!

Val was and still is an amazing hostess. She had worked in a fish and chip shop in Ascot in her youth and can still turn out the most amazing British-style fish and chips served in newspaper to a crowd. It was at one of those fish and chip parties that we would meet John and Chris Gould and continue adding more links to our friendship chain. I clearly recall John Gould, as he was introduced, cautioning us in a voice loud enough for Max to hear, "Don't talk about the war." Everyone, with the exception of Chris who has had to put up with her husband for almost 60 years, laughed at the humour—no one harder than Max—and it was through that warped, British sense of humour that we share that we became such close friends.

In time, we would meet the Hills who were tennis players which was a bonus. Heather played for Canada in many international tournaments, so she is a bit out of our league. Early on, we also met their neighbours, the Goddards, and through Marie, the Jollymores. The Jollymores are a culinary team who could knock Martha Stewart into a cocked hat. They hold the most spectacular theme dinner parties for up to forty

Monsieur et Madame Jollymore in their French Bistro.

Visiting artist, "Renoir" at Jollymores' French Bistro

people, which through the décor, music and food transport one straight into a French Bistro by the Seine or a romantic Italian Trattoria.

Up until that point, all the friends we had made were British. It wasn't planned but just the way it evolved. It is understandable that for immigrants there is an exigency to seek out those who can relate to their yesterdays. One often hears criticism of different races immigrating and not intermingling, but for many years we could be seen as guilty of that, and poor Moe Jollymore had to tolerate being referred to as "the token Canadian" at all our dinner parties.

But, it was the Jollymores who were responsible for introducing us to yet another couple of Brits—Ian and Mary Rose—so we didn't feel too sorry for Moe. He sort of brought it on himself.

More damn Brits! We just couldn't seem to get away from them.

The Hills were and still are, in their late eighties, real adventurers. Patrick and Heather built a 42 ft-boat in their back yard—quite the feat for an English couple—and along with their children, sailed it across the Pacific and up to Alaska. Heather obviously had more faith in her non-swimming husband than I could have mustered in my husband, the navigation officer!

Patrick is the man who first inspired me to write my life story. At the age of 89, he is writing his sixth book, but Heather wishes he would give writing a break because she says that sitting for hours on the computer has caused him to become less nimble on the tennis court. Men of 89 are just not what they used to be in the old days!

Returning to the story of my dismal life, January was extremely hard for me. I kept myself busy making the curtains and setting up the baby's room, but weeks went by when I did not see a soul to speak to except the check-out girl at Safeway on Kingsway. I walked up Joyce Road most days just for something to do and to experience a little human contact. I have no memory of that street beyond greyness, and it still remains a blur because when one is faced with that depth of loneliness, one doesn't see shapes or outlines, only a colourless, all-encompassing shroud into which one would like to disappear and never emerge.

I became a little more aware of local current events, through reading the local paper, but my more vivid memory is not of what was happening around me, but that the Vancouver Sun was delivered by a boy with the unforgettable name of Randy Mann. Randy men in England were those who were best avoided. That was when I first learned that one had to be careful of subtle language differences in my adopted country.

I had bought a television from Wosks Warehouse emboldened by a daily advertisement in the paper—televisions in excellent working order for as little as $10.00. I chose one which required a table which we didn't own and could not afford, so John bought a cheap package of legs and screwed them into the bottom. The set had a serious flaw in that we couldn't watch it without using a broom handle jammed in place by a chair to keep the on switch in the on position. Because that was largely a two-man operation, watching T.V. wasn't an option for me in John's absences. Four months later, I bought a brand new one which I couldn't help pointing out was still markedly cheaper than the Zenith Circle of Sound record player. It was a magnificent piece of furniture on the top of which one could display photographs or family heirlooms if one happened to own any.

Since John had been hankering after a set of Encyclopedia Britannica, he now felt justified in spending the money to balance out my expenditure on the new television, so he couldn't believe his luck when a salesman knocked on the door. The salesman couldn't believe his luck either as John made the $10.00 down payment with monthly payments of $17.50, for years to come. From then on, people were at least able to ascertain that he was an intellectual tugboat deckhand.

I wrote copious letters to family and friends at home, implying that we were having a whale of a time, and read and reread letters from them. I knew that John's mother loved to tell stories to anyone who would listen, about how well her son was doing in Vancouver—that's what parents of sons who have emigrated tend to do—so I felt it best to perpetuate the lie. Meanwhile, I was dragging around a heavy weight which prevented me from doing anything constructive. I lacked concentration and motivation, and in a world of nothingness, I went to bed, day after day, just to avoid those endless hours of nothingness. I became invisible and emotionally disconnected from the world. At night, I felt imprisoned, and my mind turned to dark thoughts. I now know that I was suffering from severe depression without ever putting a name to it.

I was unable to have any contact with John while he was at sea. After he had left, I would not hear from him again until he arrived at the dock, two to four weeks later, and phoned to say he was coming home. I was desperately lonely but accepted that this was the life that had been thrust upon me, and I had no option but to put up with it unless I risked breaking up my marriage which I would never have contemplated. I didn't ever suggest returning home or even think of it. Looking back, I ask myself why I didn't. Had my dysfunctional family, abused childhood and the British class system taught me that I didn't deserve anything better than a living hell?

During this time, I took a driving lesson in the Pontiac Laurentian in preparation for a test which must have been as terrifying for the driving instructor as it was for me. At almost nine months pregnant, I could hardly fit my bulk behind the steering wheel, and the poor man looked extremely nervous. There had to have been some adjustments on the car since the time we had to will it over the Second Narrows Bridge, but it was still very unreliable, and I was dreading what might happen on a hill start.

John believed I needed extra practise, so we went out together with me behind the wheel. That was our third stupid move, but only the first for that month. I was driving along 41st Avenue and he was issuing confusing instructions in what I perceived to be an aggressive tone which made me nervous and were not at all to my liking. Without saying a word, I slowly drew up to the curb, got out of the car as gracefully as I could in the circumstances and started strutting determinedly along the sidewalk. When he caught up, I forced him to drive beside me for several blocks before I agreed to get back in. I refused to drive home. Despite everything, I passed my test the following week, probably because the tester was anxious to get me out of the car before I delivered.

Now, if I had dared, I could have hit the road and taken the old Laurentian for a spin. At least, I was able to pick John up when he came home towards the end of the month, but that necessitated a trip across the Second Narrows Bridge which was decidedly nerve-racking. Somehow, I managed to will the old heap over the bridge for a second time, and let 'er rip down the other side.

CHAPTER FIVE

A baby's a full-time job for three adults. Nobody tells you that when you are pregnant, or you'd jump off a bridge. Nobody tells you how all-consuming it is to be a mother—how reading goes out the window and thinking too.

— Erica Jong

LIKE MOST EXPECTANT MOTHERS, I suspect, I asked myself how one tiny infant could possibly turn our world upside-down. I had prepared. I was ready. I had studied Dr. Spock like a university textbook and reviewed it over and over again.

I realised I was going into labour when I felt queasy eating my dinner one evening close to the due date. When I felt minor discomfort, I phoned the doctor. He told me to wait until the pain was "unbearable." That was decidedly encouraging. John and I sat nervously on the bed together holding hands for the next few hours as the pain increased. I kept saying, "I don't want to have a baby." to which he would reply, "I don't want you to have a baby, either." Well, perhaps we should have thought of that earlier on in the game. Now, as I cried out in agony, the goldfish idea seemed to have a little more appeal for me too.

A few hours later, it was time to go to the hospital. If the old Laurentian could get us up the slight incline to Kingsway we would be home free because it was a relatively flat journey after that to St. Vincent's Hospital where our baby arrived at 1:25 a.m. on February 6th. Only mothers can appreciate how the actual time of their children's births sticks in their head for ever.

In those days, there was no talk of the importance of bonding. The baby was immediately whisked away so that I could get a decent night's sleep. I remained in the hospital for the next week while my baby was cared for in the nursery and was presented to me only for feeding every four hours. Today's overly concerned parents are horrified by this archaic way of doing things, but I can tell you that I thoroughly enjoyed my week-long holiday and the fact that the baby had been trained to a feeding schedule by the time I took her home.

John had found himself a good tennis partner and the weather was unusually warm and sunny for February, so he breezed in every day looking healthy and tanned. We would stare into the nursery together, and I could see in his eyes and his heart that he knew the goldfish idea had not been such a good one after all.

I was thoroughly spoiled that week with visitors arriving with flowers and gifts. We had only lived in the country for seven months so I should have been grateful for all the love and attention, but it is only on looking back in my daughter's Baby Book at the long list of people who cared enough to come to the hospital and all those who sent their congratulations that I can appreciate how fortunate I really was. One of the most touching gifts I received was a bundle of letters from my Grade Two students at Talmud Torah. I wonder how those former students, who will now be over 60-years-old, would react on learning that those letters still exist in a box of my most precious possessions. Their new teacher had asked them to write to congratulate me, but I was amused to read that my new baby's arrival had not been nearly as exciting as their recent trip to Dairyland.

John had phoned his parents the night of the birth, and I sent a card to my mother in Wales where she would learn about the birth of her first granddaughter five to seven days after her arrival. In today's world, no doubt the relatives receive minute by minute texts throughout the labour and one from the mother at the moment of birth—instant gratification precluding the joy of anticipation or surprise.

Every day, John brought in the mail with more cards of congratulation. Nothing yet could have come from Wales, so towards the end of the week I was intrigued to find a letter in my mother's handwriting. Surely, she could not have received the news and be responding so soon? No, it was a Christmas card with a short message— "Happy Christmas from your Mother and all at home." Well, it was mid-February, so perhaps it was intended for the following year.

We had laboured over a name for weeks but in the end managed to choose the only name on which we could compromise which our daughter would hate for the rest of her life. Since both of our grandmothers were called Sarah, I felt that would have been the obvious choice. John thought that it sounded too old-fashioned and besides, a knife-wielding grandmother was hardly the type of woman anyone should be named after. We called her Helen because that was a common name for little girls in England at the time. I suspect that the real reason why John liked the name was that he had fond memories of watching Rossana Podesta in the 1956 Warner Bros. Epic—Helen of Troy. What we didn't realise was that Helen was considered a very old-fashioned name in Canada, whereas Sarah had gained in popularity. I really wanted a Welsh name to preserve my heritage, but John was against the idea, so in the end I had to compromise—again. We gave her the second name of Tanya for no other reason than it had a Russian flavour, and we both loved Russian literature.

The week shot by and before I knew it we were piling back into the Laurentian with our new bundle of joy dressed to kill in the clothing that my mother-in-law had secreted into the crate of John's belongings. She slept soundly all the way home and continued to sleep for so long that I had to keep checking to make sure she was still breathing. John and I had a very relaxing lunch while reading the paper. How difficult could this be? The naysayers had it all wrong—this was going to be a breeze.

Proud Dad always formally dressed.

Three hours later, all hell had broken loose. She awoke screaming, and when John picked her up, she was so caked in diarrhoea that he threw her down on the kitchen counter and bolted. That did a lot to stop the crying. I tried everything I could think of to calm her down but so much for Dr. Spock and his answer to everything. He was a dead loss! Eventually the wailing ceased, and she fell asleep while we gathered up the full washing-machine load of soiled clothes that she had managed to create in a few hours. But the closest washing machine was at the laundromat, 20 minutes away on Kingsway. One of us had to go there immediately otherwise we would be out of clean clothes within the next few hours. Erica Jong had vastly underestimated. This was going to take an army.

I feel it is pertinent to point out that disposable diapers were not available in those days, and we had only two dozen terry cloth ones at our disposal. Helen had demonstrated, in the first few hours, that those were hardly more than a two-day supply, so from then on, there were frequent trips to the laundromat when the weather was too inclement to wash the diapers by hand and hang them out to dry on the line. Those two dozen diapers would last through all three of our children, saving, at a modest estimate, 13,000 disposable ones from the landfill.

 They say the first three weeks are the hardest and it was fortunate that John was on leave to help, otherwise I may well have joined that other poor naval wife in Lynn Creek. By the time he went back to sea, things had settled into a reasonable routine which was just as well because for the next month it was going to be an army of one.

 The Brits. always put their babies to sleep outside in the fresh air, so although the weather was decidedly nippy, as soon as Helen had been bathed and fed, I put her outside at the back of the apartment every day, rain or shine. There was no garden at the back, just a junk yard full of old metal bedsprings and weeds, leading into the back lane. I have nightmares now when I think how casual I was, but I suppose those were different days—you wouldn't leave your metal garbage can lid unsupervised today or hang your underwear on the line for fear that someone would take off with them. We realised how vulnerable our baby had been, though, when years later, a middle-aged woman in John's office told him how she used to play with a baby in a maroon buggy in the back lane of Joyce Road on her way home from elementary school. We knew, instantly, that baby had to have been Helen.

 I was busy enough with the baby that the sharp edge was taken off my loneliness in John's absences, but as usual, I spent my life either longing for him to come home or dreading the day that he would have to return to sea. I did the daily trek to Safeway and now people would stop to admire the baby, so I did have a little more human contact other than the check-out girl. Until we acquired our own washing machine, there were also other exciting communication opportunities at the laundromat.

In early June, things took a nasty turn. On examining Helen, the doctor decided that she was below average weight for her age and advised me to take her to a paediatrician.

Breast feeding was not as popular in those days, so being a man who had never had a baby or breastfed one, the paediatrician said brusquely, "If you don't want her to starve, put her on the bottle and bring her back in a week." I was upset because I didn't want to do it, but I had no one to turn to so I followed his advice. When I took her back the next week, she had put on a few ounces, and he said, "I told you so, forget the breast-feeding. Like I said, you were starving her." I cried all the way home on the bus.

It wasn't until my friend, Isobel, who had been a colleague at Talmud Torah had a baby later on that year that I heard about La Leche—a group which was struck by the importance placed on breast-feeding by early Spanish settlers in America. In 1958, they dedicated a Shrine to "Nuestra Senora de la Leche y Buen Parto—Our lady of happy delivery and plentiful milk. The words spoke profoundly of yearnings that are common to many mothers. It was a group that provided a support system even before the baby was born. I had attended pre-natal classes where one would have thought information like that would have been available, but the instructor was a single, middle-aged woman who had never had a baby and either knew nothing about La Leche or thought of it as a kooky organisation. She would have been right on board with that heartless paediatrician.

It was Isobel, also, who roused my interest in Canadian politics. That was the year of Trudeaumania, the nickname given to the excitement generated by Pierre Trudeau—father of Justin. Love him or hate him, no one can deny that he was charismatic and stirred up the country like no other political figure had before him. Women adored him—seeing him as a sex symbol, and young people everywhere recognised him as a man for their time. He became leader of the Liberal Party of Canada in June 1968 and would be the third longest serving Prime Minister after succeeding Lester Pearson. We watched the results of the election with Isobel and her husband, John, and remember feeling the same kind of elation that we would later experience at the inauguration of Barack Obama in 2008.

Despite the bottle feeding, the doctor was still concerned about Helen's lack of weight-gain. After the first week on the bottle, she had reverted to her normal pattern, so the doctor told me to take her to the hospital for observation. I hadn't understood that I was expected to leave her there for a few days. I don't remember who cried the most when I handed my baby over to a nurse. I was not only feeling wretched about leaving her alone but convinced that they would find something seriously wrong with her.

When I got home, the apartment felt so empty, and I had never felt so deserted. I just longed for a mother figure or any other human being to help me through. I made myself a cup of tea and a piece of toast wondering how much worse things could get. I turned on the T.V. Bobby Kennedy had been assassinated.

I will be forever grateful to a Nurse Livingstone who worked at St. Vincent's Hospital at the time. She was a real mother to Helen; she developed such a bond with her and kept her happy. She was also the one who, just by chance, discovered that Helen had been born with hip dysplasia. It is not an uncommon condition and easily fixed if discovered at birth, but Helen was then four months old, so it was going to take about ten months to correct and require a cast and ongoing visits to the hospital. It was a relief, in one way, that her health was otherwise robust, but we were upset more for John's father who had been born with a dislocated hip and would be devastated to hear that it may have been a heredity condition. We had no choice but to tell him, but we eased his pain by telling him that the doctor had said that it was just a coincidence. Since no other future grandchildren or great grandchildren have been born with the condition, it probably was.

I can't remember how long our baby was in the hospital. When I picked her up, I was shocked and upset to see her in a cast from her upper chest down to her feet, but she had already adjusted to it and seemed quite content. She was brought down from the ward by Nurse Livingstone who had tears in her eyes as she handed Helen over.

Nurse Livingstone, with Helen in plaster cast.

Phew! she had certainly put on weight. The cast weighed more than she did. We now had to adapt to the difficulties of having a child almost completely encased in plaster. Within days, John had discovered that the cast was quite handy—Peter still remembers how John would casually prop her up on the back of the couch without any other support.

CHAPTER SIX

Sometimes, the appropriate response to reality is to go insane.

— Philip K, Dick

MY HUSBAND REALISED THAT I was ready for the psychiatric ward. He knew I was lonely and desperately in need of human contact. Communication only with the Safeway check-out girl and my laundromat acquaintances just couldn't cut it anymore, so we had handed in our notice at the beginning of June and were moving back to the West End where we had rented a two-bedroom apartment which was old but very acceptable. Alex De Cimbriani's apartment on which we had made the down payment was still not renovated.

There was a slight glitch in that John's mother, anxious to see her first granddaughter, had arranged to fly out from England the day after Helen was discharged from the hospital. She didn't know that she would be involved in a move within days of touch-down. This would be our fourth move within the year, so at least we were getting proficient at it. Other than the baby trappings which were scant compared to children's needs today, we had not acquired any more stuff beyond the infamous "Three Room Group." the vast book and record collection—now including Encyclopedia Britannica, the new

T.V., the boards and cement blocks and, if I can be so bold as to mention, the controversial Zenith Circle of Sound record player.

I vividly remember seeing my mother-in-law, Molly, coming through the arrivals gate at the airport. It had been her first flight ever, and I knew that she had been dreading it. With no idea when we might take the baby to England, she had forced herself to overcome her fear of flying. My mother had not shown the slightest inclination to visit. She was probably still writing her Christmas cards. When Molly saw Helen lying on her tummy looking like a baby turtle she was overcome. Apart from the emotion of seeing her grandchild for the first time, I knew she was thinking about John's father's life-long impediment and wondering if Helen would suffer the same fate.

I don't remember too much about the move, but I have a suspicion that the friend of the dodgy car salesman may have been involved which would have demonstrated again that we were slow learners. I expect we also relied on our friends who were happy to see us returning to the West End. It was handy to have the extra and willing pair of hands to care for Helen while we packed boxes and loaded up the furniture. Once we were settled in our semi-basement suite on Nicola Street, I felt a slight sense of relief.

We had arranged to have Helen baptised while her grandmother was in Vancouver. While we are not in any way religious, we knew it was important for Molly. The ceremony was to take place at St. Paul's Anglican Church and Molly, in her element, arranged an afternoon tea—British style. Helen looked splendid in her christening gown with its plaster cast underlay. I had made it from the material left over from my $30.00 wedding dress. Jacquie, Colin, and Marie were to act as godparents, and we had assembled a jolly crowd of "stragglers" to walk to the church. I had a momentary feeling that my life might be taking a slight turn for the better. What did I know?

As soon as the holy water touched Helen's head, she wasted no time in letting us know how she felt about the Anglican Church. She screamed bloody murder. She had become such a placid baby and rarely cried so her reaction was unexpected. She hollered as if she was being tortured, and she continued wailing on and off for the next four hours until she cried herself to sleep. My nerves were in shreds. Everyone's nerves were in shreds. To say the party was a disaster would be an understatement. Everyone went home exhausted, and we three fell into bed leaving the remains of the largely uneaten British afternoon tea congealing on plates all around the apartment.

The smiles don't tell the real story of the christening.

It was a beautiful August, and I was glad to have my mother-in-law's company. Every morning, we put Helen on a patch of grass outside the living room window to ensure that she got her dose of fresh air. In the new apartment, we could keep a close eye on her, so there was no risk that someone would take off with her. We spent every afternoon at English Bay or walking around Stanley Park. My mother-in-law had come for six weeks, but I could tell that she was not too enamoured with Vancouver and was home-sick within the first two weeks. I would never have let on that I was desperately home-sick too and that her presence and her stories of home had magnified the feeling, but she obviously knew. I heard later from several sources that she had gone back to England telling everyone how worried she was about me and how unhappy I was.

Our little turtle smiling through adversity.

Before Molly left, we had decided to investigate the possibility of buying a house. Even though I was much happier to be back in the West End, John felt it was time to move closer to those mountains that had supposedly lured him to Vancouver in the first place. In order to save enough money for the deposit, we realised that I would have to look for work, so at the same time, I applied to the Vancouver School Board, but there were no vacancies for elementary school teachers, and as it was getting very close to the start of the new term, I had put it out of my mind.

On the first day of school in September, I received a 7.00 a.m. call to say there was a class without a teacher at David Livingstone School on 23rd Avenue, off Main Street. Why didn't I have the courage to say that I was in an impossible situation? Was it a sign of weakness or strength to feel such a sense of duty? Reflecting on that dilemma, I have no doubt about what I should have done or what I would do today.

John was at sea, I had no one to look after Helen, and I had no idea where the school was located. Nevertheless, I got myself ready, packed up food and clothing for the baby, bundled her into the buggy and pushed her around to the apartment where John's tennis partner lived—I vaguely knew his wife. As Marie and Audrey were working girls, my only option was to knock on her door, tell her I was desperate and ask her if she could take the baby for the day. She was still in bed, but her husband said he would look after the baby until his wife got up and he was sure she wouldn't mind. Phew! Less than two hours later, I found myself in front of a class of Grade Two students with not a clue what I was going to do with them for a whole day without any plans, in a system that was entirely different from what I had been used to.

The Grade Four teacher, Helen, in the adjoining portable classroom, helped me through that first day giving me speed lessons on Cuisenaire rods that were used for math, and the Initial Teaching Alphabet which had recently arrived from England as an innovative method of teaching reading and writing. I had no experience of either.

The Initial Teaching Alphabet had been invented by James Pitman—grandson of Isaac Pitman, the developer of shorthand, and used symbols for 44 letter sounds. After my trial with so called innovative methods back in Bristol, I was a little sceptical and for good reason. It was a disaster—some people called it lunacy. Within a few years, we had managed to produce classes of children on both sides of the Atlantic who could hardly write or spell. The Initial Teaching Alphabet was abandoned after a few years, and we reverted to the old-fashioned method that had worked for the majority of children for years, until the next fad came along.

Following the frantic start to my new job, things didn't improve for three more weeks until John came home on leave. I had to bend the arm of the tennis player's wife to look after Helen until John turned up. By that time, she had become attached to her and was enjoying the little extra income, so she agreed to be the baby-sitter in the weeks that John wasn't home and able to care for Helen.

I wasn't entirely enamoured with my job. In fact, I would go so far as to say I disliked my job intensely. Along with my anxiety about leaving Helen with a relative stranger, perhaps the isolation of the portable classroom away from the main school and surrounded by a treeless, grey expanse of gravel had something to do with it.

My colleague in the adjoining portable surprised me one day by asking, "Do you ever feel like driving straight on past the school and not stopping?" That was exactly how I felt, so I assumed that my lack of enthusiasm must be written all over my face, but then she continued "I feel like it every day, and tomorrow, if I am not here, you'll know I have had the courage to do it." From that day on, knowing that we had been experiencing similar feelings, we formed a bond, and by supporting each other, we managed to drag ourselves through each day.

There is no doubt that my circumstances caused me to have a poor attitude, and on looking back, I know I didn't do the best job that I could have done with those children. They were not as easy to deal with as the class at Talmud Torah, so I often lacked the patience required.

My protective nature, however, came to the fore on one memorable occasion. The children were running relay races across the gravel yard during the P.E. class when a hefty, older boy ran right across between the students, knocking one of the little girls right off her feet. I raced up to him, called him a thoughtless oaf and landed a punch to his shoulder that would have won the admiration of a heavyweight boxer. Instead of carrying on to school, that big oaf ran home and appeared moments later with his intimidating mother. Her menacing demeanour made me believe that she was preparing for a fist fight, but she obviously sized me up and thought better of it. She gave me a dressing down in some colourful language and stomped into the school to report me to the headmaster. When he called me into his office, he gave me a warning, but I could sense that he was all too familiar with the boy in question and tried to disguise his amusement. I would have lost my job in this day and age. That boy would be over sixty-years-old by now. I wonder if he remembers the teacher who landed the Mohammed Ali hook to his right shoulder? I wonder if he experienced a life of trauma because of it? I would apologise if I met him. It was not really a teacher-like thing to do.

Towards the end of September, I had to take Helen back to the hospital to have her cast changed. This meant leaving her again for a couple of nights. As usual, John was at sea, so having dropped her off, I was faced with returning to an empty apartment to worry about her alone. The cast was to be replaced the next morning and she was to remain in the hospital for another night for observation.

Around two o'clock the following day, I was called to the school office to answer what I was told was "an urgent call from the hospital." With my heart in my mouth, I raced across the playground assuming the worst. The nurse on the other end of the phone informed me that Helen was in such distress that I should come to pick her up immediately. Instead of telling the secretary that I had an emergency and had to leave, a sense of duty sent me back to the classroom to complete the teaching day.

I drove like a maniac to the Children's Hospital—then on West 59th. It had opened in 1933 as the Crippled Children's Hospital, but in 1947 had been renamed Children's Hospital to "exemplify the growing awareness that children aren't defined by their illnesses"—an early and sensitive move towards political correctness.

Helen was indeed in distress, likely because the cast had been changed to hold her legs in a different position from the one they had been held in for the last four months, causing her what must have been unbearable pain. She screamed all the way home, and I remember turning on the windshield wipers because my vision was obliterated, not realising it wasn't raining. I made my way back to the bleak apartment in the West End where Helen eventually cried herself to sleep at 2 a.m. It took her three days to recover from the pain. It has taken me years!

On weekends when John was on leave, we scoured the North Shore consulting Real Estate agents and going to Open Houses. We fell in love with a brand-new house at the top of Mountain Highway, but the price of $24,000 was just out of our price range. After weeks of searching, we settled for a newly built one in Richmond as far away from the mountains as one could get. The price was $21,500 which we knew we could afford if the vendor was willing to wait for us to make the down payment until my salary was paid at the end of the month. Having secured the purchase, we handed in our notice at the apartment and prepared to move for the fifth time in seventeen months.

Just for comparison, the price that we paid for our new home was around double our combined salaries. Estimating that an average couple today might be earning a sum of $150,000 and I appreciate that the vast majority are not, $300,000 would hardly be a down-payment in Vancouver these days. Even in rural Lions Bay, in 2021, it would be impossible to buy a fixer-upper house for much less than $1.75 - $ 2 million. We have always been the lucky generation in so many ways.

CHAPTER SEVEN

And she has made a magic so that it is always winter in Narnia—always winter, but never gets to Christmas.

— C.S. Lewis

As we moved from our apartment in the West End in December and drove through Vancouver, I was reminded of that scene where Jadis, the White Witch had waved her magic wand and turned Narnia into winter for a hundred years. The trees and bushes were covered in a thick layer of sparkling frost hanging like folds of lace, the snow-lined streets were ice rinks on which cars were skating in circles, and people were bundled up like the Inuit in the Arctic, their breath turning to ice crystals as they exhaled. I don't remember how we managed to get the removal truck all the way to our new home in Richmond, but I still have a vivid picture of wheels spinning out of control on solid blue ice as we manoeuvred it up the slightest slope.

It should have been a thrill to move into our first house on Seabrook Crescent with all the associated smells of newness, but it was so bitterly cold that we were unable to fully appreciate our good fortune. The floors were of wood throughout, the picture windows all single glazed and without coverings to mitigate the freezing temperatures. We had to bundle up in coats, scarves and gloves in the house to keep warm. The gas furnace churned away endlessly, and John began to worry that if the payment of $187.13c. on our $17,000 mortgage at 8% wasn't going to reduce us to financial ruin, the heating bill surely would.

Our first house in Richmond—the cheapest new house available.

The temperature dipped to minus 18.3 degrees the next day —"cold enough to freeze the balls off a brass monkey." I had always believed that to be one of John's vulgar sayings, but it is a nautical reference to the use of a tray called a monkey which held cannonballs on warships in the sixteenth to eighteenth centuries. Apparently, in freezing temperatures, the tray would contract causing the balls to fall off. John decided it was time to protect his bodily parts from contracting and falling off by piling on yet another layer of clothing, but he was clearly concerned about the consequences of returning to sea in mid-January. Later that month, the temperature plunged to minus 23.3 degrees Celsius.

Taking advantage of only having to pay mortgage interest of $113.12c for the first two months, we splashed out on floor to ceiling drapes. It was a wise move because the frigid weather continued through January and February with below average temperatures and 132.3 cm of snow falling on 27 days. We couldn't really afford them so bought them with a down payment of $40.00 and monthly payments of $21.46, ignoring

John's father's dire warnings not to buy anything on the H.P.—hire purchase, or as he called it—"the never never."

The weather was a huge challenge for me when I returned to David Livingstone School in the first week of January, because I was now faced with the steep hill on Fraser Street every day. John, never having had much confidence in my driving skills, worried that I would not make it, but apart from having to call a tow-truck a few times—once when I ran out of gas which he will never ever let me forget, —nothing too dramatic occurred.

The biggest challenge had been trying to find day-care for Helen when John returned to sea. A neighbour, looking for some extra cash, agreed to take her, but after the first week when Helen was obviously unhappy and the neighbour's and my nerves were frayed, we knew we had to find a more permanent solution. We advertised for a baby-sitter to come to the house and that is when we found a lovely, older lady who became our saviour. She had three young boys and was delighted to have a little girl in her life whom she treated as if she were her own.

Vi is now in her nineties and living on Saltspring Island, but we have kept in touch as both our families have grown, with news of grandchildren and, in her case, great grandchildren. I should mention that Vi had not been John's first choice when we interviewed several potential candidates. He was keen to hire the busty blond who applied, and he was rather disappointed when I put the kibosh on that idea.

Sometime during January, Helen returned to the hospital to have her cast removed. This time, she didn't suffer the kind of discomfort that she had previously. The treatment was still not complete, because she then had to be fitted with Dennis Brown boots and a bar to keep her legs apart. She had never been able to sit up because of the cast, but she had become skilled at dragging herself and her hunk of plaster around the floors at rapid speed, developing the upper-body strength of an Olympic swimmer. We had to bind the bar with padding to protect the floors. When the cast was removed, we expected that it would take her months to physically catch up with other children her age, but within two weeks she was standing up unaided and walking steadily within a month.

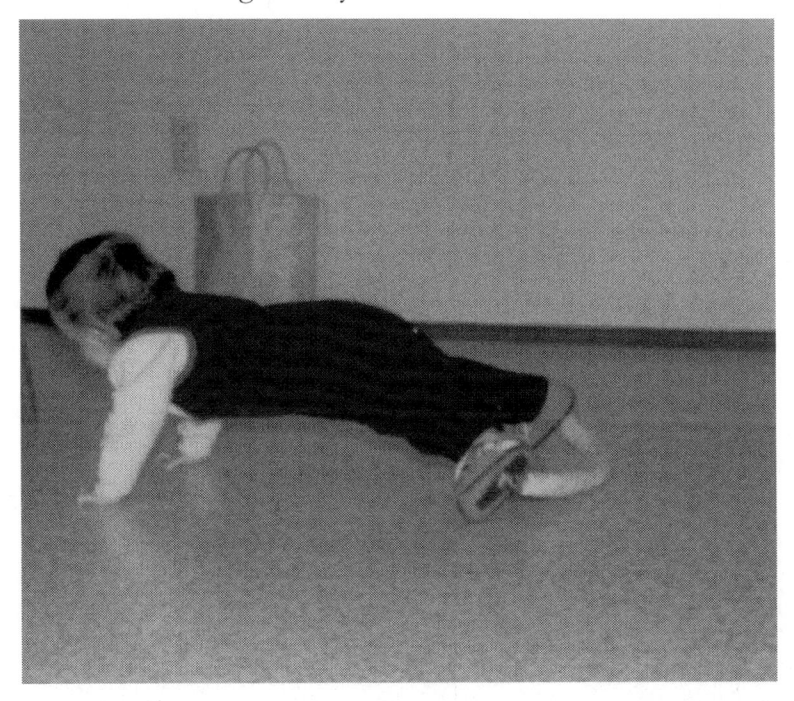

Morning push-ups in her Dennis Brown boots

Once March came, we turned our attention to landscaping the property. In an attempt to improve on the topography of Richmond, we built a rockery in the front yard. That involved numerous trips up the Squamish Highway in search of rocks. It is ironic that in the future we would make our home along that highway, and while attempting to landscape the property, wish that we could rid ourselves of rocks.

John had discovered an endless source of free wood at Seaspan which he put to use building structures in the back garden. No one else had a magnificent arbour, a sandpit, a boardwalk the whole length of the vegetable patch and a garden shed all constructed from the remains of old Seaspan barges, and no one who knows John now will be surprised to hear that old habits die hard.

We had arranged to fly to England to attend John's sister's wedding that summer—I am not sure how we had saved enough money to do it—but we had booked with a cheapo airline called Nation Air—better known as Nation Scare. We were very lucky to be able to return to England so soon, and our families were thrilled. Having something so exciting to look forward to made my job at school seem far less onerous, and with the landscaping project to get stuck into, as well as the ability to get to know the neighbours once the weather had finally warmed up, the spring flew by.

The neighbours were friendly and mostly couples of our age with young children. On the May long weekend, one family organised a group picnic to Cultus Lake up the Fraser Valley and invited us to join them. We prepared our picnic—a few egg sandwiches and a flask of tea, adding a couple of apples for good measure, and off we drove.

For half an hour after we arrived at the designated spot, we watched in amazement as the other two couples carried their picnic supplies to the beach—coolers the size of an English fridge, barbecues, chairs, sun umbrellas, blow-up sun beds and water toys, wind protection barriers, —literally everything but the kitchen sink. We sat there self-consciously eating our egg sandwiches and having a nice cup of tea while the smell of barbecued steaks wafted across the beach. Suddenly, there was an almighty crack—John, finding it too uncomfortable to sit on the ground, had gone through the lid of the ice-chest and fallen in on top of the marshmallow-surprise dessert which was more of a surprise than the creator had anticipated. That was our first and last picnic Canadian style.

Colin and Marie had bought a posh home high up in North Vancouver. It had a pool, so we spent many weekends there, often staying the night rather than making what John called, "the long trek back to Richmond." They were expecting their first baby, and she arrived in plenty of time to witness the historical landing on the moon the following month.

By the time my term had ended in June, the garden had been completed with lawns and shrubbery and wooden structures from one end to the other. Our front rockery was much admired by the neighbours, and I believe we started a trend to add some much-needed optics to the flat Richmond landscape.

My old college friends, Margaret and Tom, drove out from Swan River, Manitoba that summer. They had immigrated to Canada a year before us, but why they ended up choosing such a back-water is a mystery. Tom was a vet so I suppose he opted for a place where he could minister to farm animals as opposed to house pets. I'm guessing. I have no idea why they ended up there, and perhaps Swan River has much more to offer than I am aware of. They came with their little boy, Richard, who was four months older than Helen. I think they may have eventually chosen to move to B.C., but Tom would have been required to take more exams to qualify. I have never really understood why so many professional qualifications are not accepted federally across the board. What sense does it make to be qualified to work in one province but not in another?

Soon after their long drive home, they began to think of returning to England and the following year they did just that, settling in the idyllic Somerset countryside where we had been in college together. In her first letter, Margaret went into raptures about the picturesque old cottage that they had bought. I imagined roses around the door and a real English garden filled with Michaelmas daisies and hollyhocks. I was green with envy.

By Christmas, that lovely old cottage had become a draughty barn with no form of heating, wind whistling through the cracks and ice covering the inside of the windows every morning. Margaret believed that the damp conditions were a threat to her children's health. They were back in Canada within the year, realising it had been a costly mistake. I didn't want to hear that.

I had made some friends at the school with whom we socialised on occasion. One couple was quite taken by a larger-than-life-size model of a tall, blond haired, well-endowed young lady that John had painted. It was the "nudes on black velvet" era, but not seeing the irony, he thought those were a little crass, so his painting had been done on canvas with a black background.

He had taken up painting nudes while at sea, using centrefolds from copies of Playboy that were popular amongst the all-male crews, and continued the hobby. It required a little imagination on his part because of the staples in the navel and the airbrushed nipples and nether regions. The couple asked if they could buy his latest masterpiece to hang at the foot of their bed which sounded a little kinky to me.

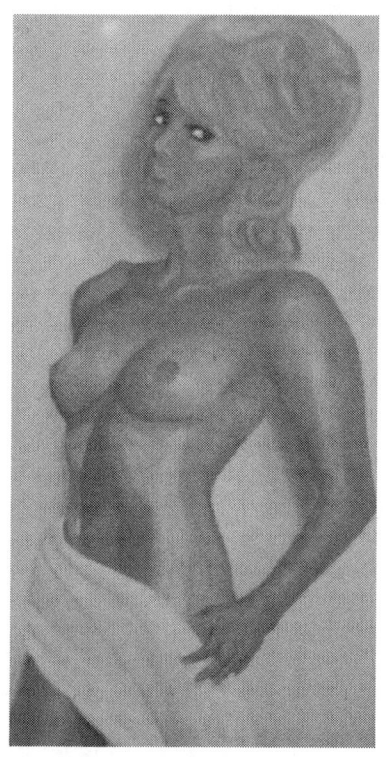

One of "Renoir" Dudley's earlier works. Helen's comment—"lady no clothes"

The friend, Shirley, died very soon after that from taking some of her husband George's medication to which she was allergic. She was a young woman with a one-year-old child. I had only ever attended one other funeral—my grandfather's—but to experience the death of a colleague in her twenties seriously affected my already faltering regard for my adopted country.

I have often wondered about the painting of the six-foot blonde nude that John left behind in England with his parents. I believe he was expecting he might see it as we wandered around the Tate Modern, one day, but my search has been focussed on junk shops in back alleys.

I had asked for a transfer to a school closer to Richmond for the following September. The winter driving had been challenging, and we believed that the past one was typical of what we could expect. I was assigned to Douglas Annexe between Fraser and Knight and looked forward to having a fresh start on our return from England.

CHAPTER EIGHT

Absence is a house so vast that inside you will pass through its walls and hang pictures in the air.

— Pablo Neruda

ONLY THOSE WHO HAVE experienced the joy of travelling home to a place that one never had any desire to leave will understand how I felt the day we boarded the plane for Britain. As we were approaching Gatwick Airport circling over those green fields that I had missed so much, I wept buckets, attempting to stem my tears. The longings that I had managed to suppress for two years issued forth in rivers of emotion.

People often say that returning home after a long absence can be disappointing—that everyone and everything will have changed and that you may have changed the most. Perhaps John felt that, because he was the one who had been so anxious to turn his back on England in the first place, but for me nothing had changed, and I was so deliriously happy to be home with six weeks to enjoy all that I had left behind. I became reenergised, as I felt the shroud under which I had been living falling away and dissolving like mist in the warmth of the sun.

John's parents were overjoyed to see that Helen's treatment had been successful. Harold had been left with the emotional scars of a dislocated hip that had never been treated. All his life, he had been self-conscious about his limp, and feeling responsible for Helen's condition, he had worried that he may have inflicted that on his grandchild.

It felt so good to be part of a family again, and I no longer had to hide my real self behind a veil. We steered clear of conversation which may have given Molly an opportunity to speak of what she had observed of my mental state on her visit to Canada the previous year.

Helen got her first experience of Molly's three-tier cake tin which would be one of the highlights of all future grandchildren's visits to Henley for years to come.

A later family picnic surrounding the three-tier cake tin which was always full.

It was a busy time with the preparations for Sue and Lyn's wedding. We were caught up in the excitement of shopping trips to Reading to purchase outfits, visits to florists, caterers and photographers and the inevitable trips to Marks and Spencer's. Molly had been more successful in persuading her daughter to have a "posh" wedding, so John and the other men had to be fitted out for morning dress.

With all immediate arrangements under control, we then drove to Wales to visit my family and introduce Helen to her other grandmother. My mother had known for months that we were coming, and we had asked her to try to borrow a crib, a highchair and a stroller for Helen as Molly had automatically done without being asked. My mother was delighted to see us but had made no effort to organise anything. It was heart-breaking to see what greeted us when we went into the bedroom; the bed was in the same state as we had left it two years prior. The same crumpled sheets were still there, and cobwebs criss-crossed the bedhead. She made no apologies, and we realised what our leaving the country had done to her—she had fallen into a deep depression. I, being her only daughter, felt that I had abandoned her.

Scouting around the neighbourhood, we quickly found everything that Helen would require, so it would have been easy for my mother to have prepared, but her mental state had crippled her.

Grandma Jones had thrown her volcanic fit over Uncle Philip's wedding the previous year, and had fled Oakdale—her home since 1909. We drove to Cwmbran to visit her, and Auntie Blodwen who was still clinging to her perceived but non-existent role as head of a family that had always taken great pleasure in ignoring her. Since I had last seen her, she had gained enough weight to more than fill an outsized armchair, and I couldn't help thinking that she bore an uncanny resemblance to Jabba the Hutt.

It was heart-breaking for me to see my grandmother looking so unlike her feisty self. I couldn't believe that this shadow of a person was the same woman who had terrorised two generations. She was so gentle and kind and so proud to meet her first great-grandchild.

She hobbled across to the fireplace and picked up a music box from the mantel that I had brought back for her from Switzerland years before. Winding it up, she said, "I have played this every single day since you have been gone, our Rosie," Hearing the haunting sounds of Edelweiss emanating from that carved box, coupled with memories of how she had verbally abused me in childhood, I was so overcome with emotion that I had to make my escape into the garden.

We spent a couple of weeks at Oakdale, my old home in Wales, while I relived my childhood through Helen's eyes, as she was introduced to the animals on the farm and was excited to collect the eggs from the henhouse. It was so good to reconnect with my cousin, Haydn, with whom I had grown up, and laugh about the good and bad old times. He was still an avid gardener, and Oakdale had become quite a show place. He had purchased a green-house and was growing bedding plants for his own garden and for other people's properties in the neighbourhood. I discovered that like me, he had regrets about the moles and rabbits that he had taught me to kill in our childhood. When I told him that I now found it impossible to kill a slug, he mentioned how his road to repentance involved sparing the lives of battery chickens which could no longer produce enough eggs and saving old ewes from the slaughterhouse. The rescued sheep were useful in keeping the grass mown in the fields and the orchard, and the chickens were housed in a huge pen where they still produced enough eggs for the household and a few extra for neighbours in exchange for the cash to buy more food for his adoptees.

We returned to Henley a week before the wedding to get involved in the final arrangements. The house was full of people including relatives from France whom we had never met. In such a tiny house, we were all falling over each other, and it seemed to be nothing but eating and clearing up in time for the next meal. It had always amazed me how Molly had calmly and efficiently produced such gourmet meals and a continuous supply of baked goods from her four-foot square scullery—too small to be designated as a kitchen. She certainly could have given lessons to the Canadians in their arena sized ones.

The wedding was a splendid affair. Molly had bought Helen a beautiful yellow dress to match the bridesmaids' outfits and she managed to wangle her way into many of the photographs. John loves to tell a story about his randy, old Uncle Eric chasing me around the churchyard, but that is pure fiction. Uncle Eric just took me behind a bush to take my photograph because he was impressed with my hat that I had bought for a quid because it was faded from being in a shop window for many years. John's Mum was so proud of her husband and her "wonderful son" dressed to kill in their rented suits.

It wasn't until we saw the photographs that we realised that the bridegroom's trousers had somehow got mixed up with his father-in-law's. Lyn, the bridegroom, was wearing those with the one shortened leg exposing his entire sock while Harold had one trouser leg completely draping over his shoe. Fortunately, all eyes were on the bride, so no one had noticed.

We had been so dismissive of Canadian television when we first emigrated, believing that British television was far superior. We were sadly disappointed. The programs that we had found hilarious as we had grown up had been replaced with others that seemed lame. We were, however, glued to the set on July 21st for the Apollo 11 moon landing and Neil Armstrong's first steps on the moon which was an unbelievable feat at that time, but 50 years later has not been repeated. The other news that was gripping the population at that time was the rioting that had broken out in Derry, Northern Ireland—the first major confrontation of The Troubles which would become headline news for years to come.

On the lighter side, Bob Dylan had returned to the stage, after three years of semi-retirement following a near fatal motorbike accident in 1966. He had attracted a crowd of 150,000 fans at a pop concert on the Isle of Wight where he sang some of his greatest hits including Mr. Tambourine Man, Like a Rolling Stone, and It Ain't Me Babe—we missed it.

But it was wonderful to catch up with our local friends again—many of them by then married with children on the way. Our level of maturity had not undergone a marked change, however, and we soon fell into the old habit of meeting up at the Rainbow—our favourite pub—and then carrying on to our best man's house in Goring to play another round of "Tap, Tap," that childish game that had afforded us such amusement in our youth.

None of John's old school friends had left the area, and it felt so good to be a part of the group again. As I typed this story of my life, I came across a quote by Harun Yahya to which I could relate— "I always wonder why birds stay in the same place when they can fly anywhere on the earth. Then, I ask myself the same question." I was also asking myself the same question that evening and feeling very much like an outsider looking in on a party from which I had been excluded.

Six weeks passed far too quickly and before we knew it, John's parents were driving us back to Gatwick. I had no desire to leave, but again, I didn't believe that there was an option. I numbed my brain and in a robotic state boarded the plane. I cried silently as the plane flew up over Scotland, and England became a vanishing speck. I have frequently wondered what would have happened if I had refused to get on that plane. I know I would not have taken the risk of losing John, and I believe that he would not have risked breaking up our solid marriage, but if he had gone back to Vancouver alone, would he have stuck it out? His working life was hardly a bed of roses. That moment at the airport, I realise now, could have been the turning point. My life from then on was destined to be lived in Canada—a country that would never ever truly feel like home.

Nation Scare had managed to deliver us to London unscathed, but I was still a little nervous on the return journey and with good reason as it turned out. All went well until we were flying over the Rockies, and the pilot made a rather troubling announcement. "There is no need to be concerned, but we are experiencing a problem with the landing gear; we are unable to operate the machinery to get it down." That was hardly encouraging news. Everyone immediately lined up for the toilets. The silence amongst the passengers was palpable as we all considered our individual fate. After a few minutes which seemed like hours, the pilot announced that the flight attendants had been instructed to go through emergency procedures pending a crash landing. Strong men were moved to emergency doors and all fathers were told to hold on tightly to their children. I looked for signs of concern on the faces of the crew and was not reassured; they too looked worried and were carrying out their duties in absolute silence. The next half hour was agonising, until the pilot made a further announcement: "We are attempting to get the landing gear down manually; we will keep you updated." With relief, we heard that familiar cranking sound that told us that the landing gear was being lowered, and then the pilot informed us that although it had been positioned successfully, we should prepare for a crash landing and not to be perturbed by a fleet of ambulances and fire trucks that would be standing by on the runway—easier said than done—and a few more people headed to the toilet.

That pilot should have been awarded a medal for the skill with which he landed that plane. There was a resounding bang as we hit the runway and veered only slightly off course. The fire trucks and ambulances drove beside us as we taxied to the gate. A collective sigh of relief was followed by a rustling of paper as many of the passengers retrieved their cigarettes to calm their nerves—smoking was allowed on planes in those days but had been banned throughout the emergency. Nation Scare had lived up to its reputation, but we had all survived to tell the tale.

CHAPTER NINE

Life is a series of natural and spontaneous changes, don't resist them—that only creates sorrow. Let reality be reality. Let things flow naturally forward in whatever way they like.

— Lao Tsu

I COULD HAVE WALLOWED in the "Slough of Despond" like Christian in Bunyan's Pilgrim's Progress on our return to Seabrook Crescent, but although I felt bereft, I tried to accept that this was reality, to look to the future and not feel sorry for myself. It was easier not to dwell on the happiness of the past six weeks, because we both had to return to work immediately and rehire Vi to take up her duties caring for Helen. That was the grim reality.

I was so much happier at my new school—Douglas Annexe on Borden Street. The headmistress, Myrtle Watchorn, was such a warm individual and the staff were kind and welcoming. I was relieved to have made the change, but I kept in touch with some of the friends I had made, especially Helen Kirkby who had unknowingly supported me through that first difficult year.

Helen's husband, Ken, is an artist who at the time we met was greatly influenced by the work of Andrew Wyeth whose paintings we much admire. We bought several of Ken's early works—the first one for $50.00, believing that he was destined for international fame. Like the people who have happened upon early Monet's or Picasso's and seen them sold for millions at Sotheby's, we dreamed of the day we would be in that position ourselves. It was not to be, but Ken, now eighty-years-old, is still painting, so I am not yet giving up hope. When I read the list of famous people who own his work—the Queen and Pierre Trudeau, to name two—I was rather disappointed not to see the Dudley collection mentioned.

On weekends, we often drove to North Vancouver to visit Colin and Marie and their daughter, Alexis. Because I didn't like driving and, as you have already gathered, John had an aversion to it, we often spent the weekend there and have memories of raucous dinner parties and drunken, night-time dips in the pool. It should be no surprise that when I am whining about my awful life to Chris and Tish, I forget that there was the occasional good time—I believe I may be suffering from a severe case of selective memory, and I wonder if they have the same condition.

My intention had been to spend only one year at my new school because we were hoping to have a second baby—the goldfish idea having already been scuppered by the first birth—but I was surprised that month after month our hopes were dashed until the following January. It then appeared to have worked out well after all because I would be able to leave the school in June and have some time with Helen until the new baby arrived in November.

Unfortunately, everything was against us. On May 2nd, John's union called a strike, and he suffered the indignity of being on a picket line for the next six weeks until the middle of June. But who can tell? Could being on a picket line be any worse than daily vomiting at sea? It was a worrying time financially, because we knew we would be no longer reliant on my salary after the school year ended. But things got worse—the Teachers' Union started to make mumblings about striking and sure enough, I ended up on a picket line too. Fortunately, it was only a one-day strike for teachers before the government stepped in, but sadly, that was the day that I was devastated to discover that I was about to lose my baby. John rushed me to the hospital as soon as he was released from the picket line, but it was futile.

I did not share my news with anyone, feeling that it was such a personal issue, but I have been upset to hear people criticising Meghan Markle, who has just gone through the same experience, and was brave enough to tell the world about her devastating loss. Unless one has been through it, one cannot begin to understand the feeling of emptiness and unfulfillment with which one is left. Despite what I had experienced, I returned to school the very next day, pretending to be absorbed in the discussion on the strike while concealing the fact that I was hurting both physically and mentally.

Six weeks on the picket line had been demeaning for John, so he began to wonder if he should look around for a shore job. He tried his hand at sales during his next leave, to see if he had an aptitude for it and got a job selling fire alarms. He took the training course and was told that his spiel was excellent—in other words he had a good line of bull-shit. Unfortunately, he didn't seem to be a good closer. He was doing really well on one potential sale, and the purchaser seemed on the verge of buying, but when John closed in on him more forcefully with the contract to sign, he became very aggressive and threw John out of the house bodily. Each customer was to be given a free case of coke, whether or not they made a purchase, so as John left, he shouted, "Well, you are welcome to keep the coke." To which the man replied,

"You damn well keep your f………g coke," and hurled the whole case across the lawn. John sheepishly gathered up the cans and brought them home where they went to waste because neither of us could stomach the stuff. That ended his short career as a salesman, and he decided that perhaps there were worse careers than a sea-going life.

When school ended for the summer, we thought it was time to explore Canada. Isobel and John had moved to Vernon, Mike and Audrey to Calgary and Tom and Margaret were still in Swan River. We would make our way to Manitoba, stopping along the way to visit our friends.

We were just passing through Abbotsford when I remembered the eggs boiling on the stove at home—we had been planning to eat more damned egg sandwiches—but fortunately, Vi had a key and was at home so was able to retrieve the ruined saucepan before the house burned down.

By the time we reached Chilliwack, Helen was car-sick and throwing up—happy days! We battled on to Vernon where it was so hot that a very pregnant Isobel was doing her ironing in the basement in just her bra and pants. We were all feeling the heat, Helen was miserable, I was impatient with her, and it was a ghastly visit which we cut short for our hosts' sake. Soon after that, Isobel suffered a miscarriage for which I hope we were not partially responsible.

As you have already gathered, we are slow learners so it will not surprise you to know that we persisted, arriving exhausted, hot and bedraggled in Calgary two days later. That was the year that a foolhardy decision not to spray for mosquitoes had been made. Just our luck! We, coming from Britain had never experienced anything quite like it. Within days, our bodies were just one huge mosquito bite necessitating frequent baths in calamine lotion. Every time we stepped outside, a multitude of them would ascend in a cloud from the grass, covering our red-raw bodies for a second onslaught. A game of tennis with Michael had to be abandoned when the balls disappeared into their haze. Well, now we had finally learned our lesson—Manitoba would have to wait for another day, maybe for ever. Margaret and Tom have since moved to Saskatoon, having had their abortive attempt to return to live in England in the meantime, but memories of that dreadful trip still haunt us, so we have not yet mustered up the courage to visit them in Saskatoon.

Oddly enough, on the return journey, Helen had recovered from her travel sickness, and was chatting and singing happily between naps in the back of the car. We drove home in record time—from Jasper to Richmond in less than ten hours, desperate not to miss an episode of The Forsyte Saga—the last major British serial to be shown in black and white and watched by millions around the world. That may have been the episode where Soames raped his wife, Irene, which would have been a shocking scene in those days and possibly the main reason for the show's popularity. More discerning viewers were turning their attention to the raids and bombings by the F.L.Q. [Quebec Liberation Front] leading up to the October Crisis.

The F.L.Q. was founded in 1963 to fight for Quebec independence. The members claimed to be fighting against "a capitalist system which they felt was English dominated and foreign owned." Surprise! Surprise! Things came to a head when British Trade Commissioner, James Cross, was kidnapped and held for 59 days, followed by Quebec's Minister of Labour —Pierre Laporte. Trudeau invoked the War Measures Act on October 16th—a move that had never before been carried out in peace time, but it was too late for Laporte who was found assassinated in the trunk of a car. Captured and arrested were Paul and Jacques Rose and Francis Simard who, when freed in the 80s, became contributing members of society as writers, film makers and commentators. Around the world, no one could have believed that something so horrific could happen in a peaceful country like Canada.

I had returned to school in September and not unhappily. I had a delightful class of students, and I enjoyed the staff and the support and kindness of the head. Something else that made it special was that John would come with Helen to pick me up from school every day when he was ashore, bringing me a Mr. Big chocolate bar to eat on the way home.

The following year, 1971 was to be a special year—the 100th anniversary of British Columbia joining Confederation, so preparations went into full gear almost immediately, with songs to sing, plays to perform and murals to paint.

There was a greater effort to involve Indigenous people in the 1971 Centennial celebrations, but they were still largely denied special status. Indian participation sub-committees were set up but without proper consultation. The Indigenous Bands were mainly brought in to add colour to the celebrations—what one might call window dressing. Dan George, however, a prominent B.C. Chief, was invited, again, to the Empire Stadium where a huge crowd listened to him give a memorable speech lamenting his lost culture. The Queen, Prince Philip and Princess Anne had been invited to join in the celebrations and did tour much of B.C., probably collecting numerous gifts of totem poles along the way.

On a previous occasion, in 1958—the 100th year since Queen Victoria had declared British Columbia a British Crown Colony, the Queen was presented with a 100-ft totem pole carved by a master carver—Chief Mungo Martin of the Kwakwaka'wakw Nation. Earlier on, he had abandoned carving as a protest against the banning of potlatches, but he had continued with his work when the ban was lifted in 1952.

The pole, which now stands in Windsor Great Park had been carved from a 600-year-old cedar tree from Haida Gwaii and each figure represents the mythical ancestor of a different clan. It weighed 27,000 pounds and was perhaps one of the more unusual gifts that has ever been presented to the Queen —hardly a gift for her to lug on to the Britannia. When Chief Mungo Martin was not invited to attend the ceremony, he put a curse on the pole. It is purported that the curse was later removed, but for those of us presently watching the BBC production of The Crown, we can be forgiven for believing that the curse still stands.

I have no recollection of how we included Indigenous culture into the curriculum at my school. My class was responsible for the mural that formed the backdrop for the dramatic performances, and I can only hope that it did not just feature explorers, gold prospectors and pioneers. I have to admit that in my early life in Canada, I had little knowledge of the despicable treatment that my ancestors had inflicted upon the Indigenous people.

There was an official Centennial song called Go British Columbia that was composed by Bobby Gimby—affectionately known as the Pied Piper of Canada. The song generated lots of controversy because Gimby was paid over $10,000, and the word "Centennial" wasn't even included. Others didn't like the chorus which consisted of nothing but la, la, la, la. It doesn't sound as if we got much for our money.

I have no memory of that song because our children were taught a different one which I suspect was composed by our very talented Kindergarten teacher who rejected Bobby's song outright. I can still sing the first four lines, but the rest escapes me. I thought I could depend on John who has an uncanny knack for remembering the words to every song written between the 50s and the 70s, but while he could also remember the first four lines and immediately burst into song, he, too, could only la la la la the rest. Could that song also have omitted any reference to Native culture? Perhaps it is best that we will never know.

By March, I was thrilled to find I was pregnant once more, and as long as everything went well, I would be able to complete my year at the school and look forward to the new baby in November. I kept the news to myself because I was nervous that I would be disappointed again. By June, it was obvious why I was handing in my notice, and the staff congratulated me and wished me well. I was so sad to leave, quite the opposite feeling on leaving David Livingstone earlier, but I looked forward to a break from teaching, being home with Helen and getting to know the neighbours

CHAPTER TEN

A road trip is a way for the whole family to spend time together and annoy each other in interesting new places.

— Tom Lichtenheld

JOHN'S PARENTS DECIDED THAT they would visit us that summer, so we had something to look forward to. It would be Harold's first visit, so John was quite excited to be able to show off his handiwork. Harold was a man who could put his hand to anything, so John was obviously hoping to impress him. The garden was looking quite magnificent by that stage.

His parents were as taken with our home as we had been with Jacquie and Peter's, and the fake teak feature wall was much admired as were the fake marble kitchen counters. Molly was quite in awe of the kitchen which was easily four times the size of hers in Henley. I don't think they could believe what we had accomplished in the house and garden in such a short time. We still had the disgusting "Three Room Group," but it looked marginally more presentable in our new surroundings.

John's father was a keen photographer and one of his lifelong desires was to see and photograph the Rockies. He had no idea of the distance involved, and as I have mentioned previously, we both disliked driving. Not wishing to disappoint him, however, we had pre-booked pioneer-style accommodation along the way. I don't think anything more luxurious was available in rural B.C. in 1971, and gourmet dining was definitely not an option in those days unless one had the means to book into the Banff Springs Hotel or the Chateau Lake Louise.

John had discovered that the best way to overcome his dislike of driving was to get on the road "before the rush"—to this day, he still considers any more than three other cars on the road "gridlock," and when we have finished our weekly shop at the closest mall, he sighs with relief saying, "Let's get out of this hell hole."

Setting off on our trip, we had all agreed that a 7:00 a.m. start would be reasonable. With everyone cooperating, we were all in the car ready to drive away by 6:30 a.m. when John admitted to changing the clocks. It was actually 5:30 a.m. I was thoroughly pissed off with him for the second time.

To mitigate the tension, John's Dad lit up his pipe only to be told, "No Dad, you can't smoke in the car," offending both his parents who thought John was being disrespectful. For the record, both his Mum and Dad would die of cancer some years later—his Dad from lung cancer and his Mum from esophageal cancer probably as a result of her husband's smoking. We set off smoke-free but enveloped in a steam which thickened as I recognised that this was another great opportunity to raise the subject of the record player purchase. The air didn't clear until we stopped in a sleazy café in Hope—often referred to as No Hope—for breakfast at 7.30 a.m. We had definitely made it "before the rush."

After the tension on the first day, it was a successful trip barring a few minor glitches. Smoke from forest fires in the Interior of B.C. was disappointing for a photographer, but by the time we reached the Rockies the air was clear. John's Dad had some problems with Canadian ways, but three days into the trip he figured out that a shirt and tie and his lightweight travelling suit rendered him overdressed for the occasion. He eventually removed his tie and opened the top button on his shirt to give himself that casual "Canadian look."

When asked if he would like hard or soft ice-cream, John's father who was a middle of the road kind of guy always asked for medium which confused the waitresses. Then he ordered two large pizzas—one for himself and one for Molly—something that they had never eaten in their lives. They were still eating them cold, for lunch, three days later.

Our accommodation was rather basic and small, and John's Dad who because of his limp was known to fall over, amazed us all when he tripped at the door and flew right across the room landing neatly inside an open suitcase. We have a habit in our family of doubling over with laughter when someone is hurt, especially if there is blood. Poor Harold was obviously badly injured but Molly, not exactly sympathetic, just repeated what she always said in her resigned way when Harold fell, "Oh, for God's sake, Harold, what on earth do you think you're doing? Get out of that damn suitcase!"

They were in awe when they saw the Rockies for the first time. Photographs can never do them justice. The Icefields Highway between Banff and Jasper has to be one of the most spectacular drives in the world. Molly and Harold had not been world travellers, so they were enthralled by the magnificence of it all. Their trip onto the Athabasca Glacier was something that they talked about for years. John's father was a man who was interested in, and appreciated everything. He was for ever doing research and asking questions—the best kind of guest to entertain.

He was fascinated by the length of the trains in Canada and the haunting noise of the whistle they made which he thought of as "so Canadian." On our way home, we stopped many times for him to get exactly the right photograph, racing ahead and then waiting for the train to come into view and disappear around the next bend.

John became impatient with all the starting and stopping, because the clutch was beginning to go on our "very reliable" three-year-old, English Vauxhall Viva, and for some reason he thought that driving like a maniac was going to solve the problem. The steam began to fog up the windows once again.

On our return to Richmond, we spent the next few weeks taking his parents on local sight-seeing tours, and we drove them up the Squamish Highway unaware that we would be living there much sooner than I could have imagined. The Boeing 747 had just gone into service in Vancouver so we rushed across to the airport almost every morning so that John's Dad could take "just one more photograph" of the take-off. He was also fascinated by the tugs and John's stories of his duties on them. He worked for an engineering firm—by coincidence, the one that had manufactured the mechanism for the Gastown steam clock—so engines of all sorts were right up his alley.

My father-in-law had been in close contact with Ray Saunders during the making of the steam engine for the clock, so when my in-laws came to Vancouver, we were all invited down to Ray's workshop. Harold was fascinated by Ray's skill and creativity.

Ray Saunders, now in his 80s, still repairing clocks.

By coincidence, while writing this Memoir, 50 years on, I was thrilled to see Ray, who is still in the business, featured on the front page of The Vancouver Sun. He is holding the old clock from The White Lunch, the restaurant where we first ate on our arrival in Vancouver in 1967.

I think that Molly enjoyed her stay much more than she had on her first visit. For one thing, she was seeing us in much better financial circumstances and in a home of our own. She had come with Harold this time and was able to enjoy everything through his eyes. She was able to take great delight in her granddaughter who was by then three years old and very talkative, and perhaps she believed that I seemed more settled which made her more accepting of the idea that we were in Canada to stay. I know that in those early years she was secretly hoping that I would be the one to persuade her son to come home. I still, to this day, wonder why I didn't.

The time passed far too quickly, and the parting was much more emotional because on this occasion they were having to say goodbye to their grandchild as well as us. Knowing that the new baby was on the way made it that much harder. Without knowing how we would manage it, we promised that we would fly to England the following summer.

CHAPTER ELEVEN

If you turn off the news and talk to your neighbours, you'll find that our country is far more harmonious than you're being told.

— Rob Schneider

THERE WERE FIVE FAMILIES with small children on our street in Richmond with whom we began to socialise after I had finished teaching. The disastrous picnic and the destruction of the ice-chest by that "odd English couple who thought a picnic meant two egg sandwiches and a flask of tea," had been long forgotten. We found that we had much in common. The streets were flat and the houses all side by side, so it was very safe for small children. Helen had started pre-school but most of the time enjoyed playing with her new friends.

The next-door neighbours, Ineke and John and their neighbours, Arlene and Rod, on the other side were delightful, but Ineke was an intimidating housekeeper. Friends who know us now, jokingly ask if they should take their shoes off before entering our garage, but compared to Ineke, we were hillbillies. Their home was a show place. It was the first time I had seen a child-proof fence erected around a living room. Their children, Tommy and Joyanne were only allowed to play in our sandpit if they wore gloves which were removed and washed as they re-entered the house. Ineke and John saved themselves a lot of discomfort—our floors, carpet, clothes, and the bathtub were permanently filled with sand, and each night we slept in a gravel pit.

Our neighbour, John, worked for Datsun which was the reason we soon swapped the "reliable" British lemon for a "reliable" Japanese car. As far as the engine went, we had no complaints, but the body began to rust away and my husband being inventive, started plugging the holes as soon as a new one appeared. Very soon, almost the entire body was plastic wood which held it together for quite a few more years. The rusting problem had been solved in future models, and our old neighbour would be delighted to know that we have always replaced our cars with new Datsuns—the name was changed to Nissan in 1986—and 50 years on, we still own one.

John continued to come and go for weeks at a time, but now that I was part of a real neighbourhood, life was not quite so lonely. The neighbours would congregate on the street watching the children playing and riding their trikes so there were always people to talk to. Jacquie and Peter and their two little ones were just a stone's throw across the back lane, and we kept in close touch.

The night before our second baby was born, a group of us went out to a restaurant for a substantial dinner together and then back to a home on the street to listen to music and chat until around 1.00 a.m.

One of the husbands was obsessed with the music of Neil Diamond which was blaring forth as we left the house, and I remember John saying jokingly, as I sashayed down the garden path, "Crackling Rosie won't be so crackling if she ends up having a baby tonight."

Just an hour later, we were on our way to the hospital where Alison made her appearance at precisely 3.10 a.m. only forty minutes after we had arrived in the maternity ward. My doctor, donning his rubber gloves, careened around the end of the bed just in time to catch her as she shot forth. I felt no pain at all and deduced that the way to have a baby is to be unsuspecting and completely relaxed. Crackling Rosie was still crackling way into the night.

I looked forward to another week's holiday at St. Vincent's hospital, while John held the fort at home. Again, I was showered with flowers and gifts, and John never forgot to bring me a Mr. Big chocolate bar every day when he came in with Helen who was fascinated by her little sister.

Alison had not caused any trouble during the pregnancy and birth, but she soon made her presence felt when we took her home and John returned to sea two days later. For four months, she kept me on my feet and both of us—when John breezed in intermittently—for five hours every evening, when she finally settled down and we fell into bed exhausted. During that time, we filled her with litres of Woodward's gripe water which was no help at all, and Dr. Spock was, again, a dead loss.

Woodward's gripe water was invented by William Woodward with the claim that it would settle the stomachs of fretful babies. It was marketed under the slogan, "Granny told Mother and Mother told me." Prior to the alcohol being removed, Woodward had recommended a maximum does equivalent to five tots of whiskey for an 80 kg. adult. It's a wonder that Alison didn't become a raging alcoholic. How many of us look back and believe that we must have been neglectful parents?

Thankfully, at the end of the four months, as if a switch had been turned off, Alison began to smile and has been smiling ever since despite having dealt with a severe nut allergy which came to light when she was about three-years-old. At the age of 50, she is not yet showing signs of alcoholism but there's still time!

It took us some time to discover what was causing such severe allergic reactions, and she was rushed to hospital on more than one occasion. With food allergies becoming more common, products began to be more clearly labelled, but despite that, there were many occasions when nut products had been added to food items that one would never suspect. I can't count the number of attacks she has had throughout her life, but no one will forget the panic surrounding the one she had on her wedding day, just five hours before the ceremony.

Christmas of 1970 was again spent with Colin and Marie who by that time had two children—Daniel had arrived in April—and our children would also become friends for life. Along with others we were yet to meet, they became the family we had left behind in England. Over the years, we would spend many memorable holidays together—in Canon Beach and at Seabreeze Lodge on Hornby Island—and we made it a tradition to splash out for Easter Brunch at the Vancouver Hotel. I realise how blessed we were, but Chris and Tish have never heard any of these stories because it would ruin the plot.

John had probably, by then, run out of garden structures that could be built with discarded barges so, inspired by Ken, he turned his hand back to oil painting, the subject matter then becoming far more suitable for a family man—the Royal Yacht Britannia in Vancouver Harbour, pictures of tugs, landscapes and the like. Much of his early work is still hidden away in a closet, but as with our Kirkby collection, is unlikely to turn us into billionaires.

It had been an unusually wet winter and spring, and one morning we were alarmed to find a swimming pool in our basement. Like most houses built in those days, basements were left unfinished to reduce the purchase price, so apart from having to wear boots for the next few days, it wasn't an insurmountable problem. Over the course of a week, the flood subsided and there was no permanent damage. The builder had not put in drain tile which in an area that is below sea-level was either an omission or an impossibility. John fixed the problem as best he could by surrounding the house with wide gravel paths, but we knew from watching new house foundations being constructed in rain-filled lakes that it would be only a temporary solution.

Many years later, we got a call from an agitated owner who asked us if we had ever experienced water problems in the house. By that time, the poor man had finished the basement and his furniture was floating. He lamented, "Every time I jump up and down in the corner of the house, I hear a squelching sound." John suggested that the solution might be to stop jumping up and down in the corner, and it must have been sound advice because we never heard from the unfortunate man again.

May rolled around, and as John's salary was fast approaching $10,000 per annum, we were able to book our airfares to England. I arranged to leave with the children, and he planned to join us for six weeks in July and August.

Two days before we left, Colin took John to climb the Lions for the second time. He came home raving about a small community nestled below, so not wishing to waste any time, we drove to Lions Bay the very next day.

We found an A-frame sales office where the notice now stands at Harvey Creek Bridge and within the hour, we had purchased a lot for $11,000 on Upper Bayview Rd.—some would say a rather impulsive move.

There were only two other houses on the street at the time. I went home thinking that sometime in the future—perhaps after the children had left home—it wouldn't be a bad place to live. It was heavily forested and dark which didn't appeal to me, but the views of Howe Sound and across to Vancouver Island were spectacular.

The following day, the girls and I boarded the plane for England.

CHAPTER TWELVE

Behind every angry woman stands a man who has absolutely no idea what he did wrong.

— H.B, JT.

THIS TIME, WE HAD booked flights on a reputable airline. John was not about to risk the lives of his entire family on Nation Scare, but after our last experience I was still apprehensive.

My fears were allayed, however, because of a child in the row behind us who screamed all the way to London. I completely understand how fellow passengers have the urge to kill in those circumstances, but I was full of sympathy for a mother who was wearing the shoes that I had just stepped out of; there is nothing like past experience to cause one to withhold judgement. The mother had taken her doctor's advice and drugged the child, and it was obviously having the opposite effect. That may have been when the Woodward's gripe water penny dropped for me. Alison slept peacefully in a sky-cot hung from the rack—too risky these days—and Helen played and slept beside me for the ten-hour journey. I didn't envy the jaded woman with the screaming child who, I discovered, was carrying on to Delhi.

It felt so good to be returning to what was still home to me, and I wept uncontrollably again as the plane circled above the green fields of England. I anticipated the joy on the faces of our family and old friends. That familiar lightness surged through my veins, and I was immediately reenergised.

Molly, as usual, had prepared for royalty. In a way, her life was not unlike mine—constantly living for the day her son, with his family, came home and all the time he was there, dreading the time he would leave. Except in her case, the absences were in years, not weeks. Until we had grandchildren of our own, I did not fully appreciate what a wrench it must have been for our parents to have been deprived of theirs. I really don't feel we deserve to have ours no more than 25 minutes away. They will, unknowingly, forever rekindle a sting that endures.

Helen makes friends with the baby calves back at my home in Wales.

I enjoyed my time back in Wales. Helen was four years old and loved the farm life. She was able to watch the sheep dipping and shearing, and make friends with the lambs and baby calves. I felt such sadness that my children would never grow up in the country that I had loved and enjoy the kind of experiences that had kept me grounded. My mother, as she had done with me, spent hours familiarising Helen with all the wild flowers that grew in the hedgerows, and she loved the flower-filled country lanes and searching for wild strawberries.

My wonderful old teacher, Mrs. Powell, was still teaching at Tregaer School and was delighted to include my daughter in her class, so every morning Helen and my mother, who was still the school cook, would trot off to school together along the same stretch of country lane that I had walked 26 years earlier. There was such a feeling of permanence in my life for those few precious weeks, which I knew was going to be wrenched away from me all too soon.

Reconnecting with Mrs. Powell—my old teacher in Wales.

In Henley, I had enjoyed frequent phone calls from John, but in Wales we were reduced to regular mail. It may have been 1972, but the only phone, other than at the Bradley's house across the fields—the one through which faithful old Tony had arranged my dates in my youth—was in the red telephone box a mile or more up the road. Anticipating that situation, I had brought along a bag of small change, so that I could have long conversations with John once in a while.

I was upset to read in the first letter that I received that our neighbours, John and Ineka, had listed their house for sale and were intending to move to Calgary. Only three days later, I received another letter telling me that their house had sold, "for a good profit."—a good profit in those days being around $11,000. There was something about the wording in that letter that made me a little suspicious, and sure enough, in the next letter, I learned that our house was up for sale.

A phone call was in order, one that John probably will recall with greater clarity than I. To say that I was furious would be an understatement. In the middle of the bickering, I told him that, in the circumstances, I had decided to stay in Wales and slammed down the phone. That must have been a very anxious few days for him since he had no way to contact me again unless I called him back which I had no intention of doing. I phoned my in-laws to tell them what "Molly's wonderful son" had done. They were dumbfounded, but perhaps hopeful that I would carry out my threat and bring their son home.

After three days, I relented but fully expected the sale would be off. It wasn't. John had filled the house with Ken's paintings and was actually getting offers. Knowing he had a great desire to build a home on the mountain property we had bought, I foolishly softened my stance and agreed that the sale could go ahead as long as the closing date was some weeks after we were due home in September. He gave me his word. The house sold the next day "for a good profit."

All was peace and harmony until, really missing John one evening, I walked to the telephone box. That's when he told me that he had agreed to let the new owners move into our house in August. I was speechless and left the phone swinging from its cord, as I stomped out of the telephone box and marched home. This was really a case for the divorce courts, but that bugger was so sure of my love for him that he knew I would let him get away with it. The deal was signed and there was no way out unless I carried out my threat. Believe me, I thought about it! Was I still that "Sloppy, Spineless Creature," allowing myself to be trapped by love?

I returned to Henley just before he flew into London. Harold, the children and I went to meet him. His father had dressed in a three-piece-suit for the occasion, as was his custom, so when John came through the arrivals gate, he almost fell over as did I.

We had to look twice at the man coming towards us wearing a pair of pull-on, purple-checked, polyester bell-bottomed pants and a kind of candlewick, dark purple shirt. With a back-pack thrown over his shoulder, he looked like a latent hippie ready for the Glastonbury Music Festival. I didn't doubt that he had found his new items of clothing in the bargain basement at the Bay, and they had been the only choices that were close to fitting him. That outfit has been worn by several of our children for "sixties" parties over the years, but somewhere along the way has been mislaid. That's probably just as well, as he would surely still be wearing it.

The next few weeks were frantic as we drove up and down the country visiting all our old friends—in Catterick, in York, and in Amersham. Mike and Audrey had moved back to Bargoed—from the picturesque West End of Vancouver to a home beside a man-made lake in Calgary to Bargoed in South Wales where they enjoy a prime view of a slag heap. But it was home, where their hearts had become whole, and they live there happily to this day. From Bargoed, it was just a skip and a hop to visit all the Welsh relatives. It was a whirlwind holiday and will go down in my memory as one of my happiest summers.

We had decided to have Alison baptised at Harpsden—the church where we had been married. Jane Austen's grandfather, Thomas Leigh, had been the rector there, and Jane's mother, Cassandra, had been baptised in the font in 1739. Sharing a font with Jane Austen's mother would give Alison her claim to fame. Molly was looking forward to yet another excuse for a tea party, and we hoped it would be a happier occasion than the last baptism in Vancouver.

People tell you that you remember every detail about the first baby but much less about the second, and I realise how true that is, when I can't remember all those whom we asked to be godparents. I know that Michael is Alison's godfather, but I remembered that my college friend, Ros, is a godmother only because she appears in the photographs. Whoever the other godmother is has been about as conscientious as John and I have been as godparents.

Alison wearing the same christening robe made from my $30.00 wedding dress.

Alison seemed to have no quarrel with the Anglican church and smiled and laughed through her whole dousing. It was a beautiful day in an endless summer, and although I am not a religious person in the true sense of the word, I found something very spiritual about that ceremony in the church where we had been married five years previously by the same minister.

It's an English custom to save the top tier of the wedding cake for the first baby's christening, but since the cake was stored in an attic in England when Helen was christened, Molly retrieved it for this occasion. That might be enough to turn the stomachs of North Americans who are into refrigeration big time, but when we removed the icing to redecorate that cake, it was moister and tastier than it had been five years before, and no one suffered from food poisoning.

It was a jolly party with so many of the Dudley clan and our old friends in attendance. When I look back at photographs of all the people who were there, I grieve for the brevity of life —so many of those who played such a short but vital role in our lives are no longer with us, but I appreciate that every one of them helped, in some small way, to make us who we are today.

All good things come to an end and before we knew it we were having to return to Canada. I couldn't say I was going home because someone else was now living in my home. John had found a builder in Lions Bay to construct a house for us on the lot we had bought back in May, but he was already building a house further down the road which he persuaded John to buy in exchange for the lot. The house was $2,000 more than John had received for the Richmond house—a substantial amount for a family now expecting to live on less than $10,000 per annum.

John was so excited to show us the new house. He just didn't get it. He had worked like a fiend to move everything out of our house into storage at a friend's house in South Granville, and then move it out of there to set up everything in the Lions Bay house, after tearing around the stores choosing colour schemes, plumbing fixtures, carpets and appliances. He was sure I would fall into his arms with gratitude and congratulate him for all his hard work. I didn't. I had given no input into the place at all, and I was resentful. He had told me it was so beautiful and that I wouldn't believe it. It wasn't and I didn't. I wanted to return to my own home, the one in which someone else was now living.

Helen was four-years-old and had been looking forward to seeing her old friends. Every few hours she cried, "Mummy, when are we going home?" It broke my heart. When she finally accepted that it wasn't to be, she spent hours every day living through her trauma by drawing pictures of her old friends, Tommy, Joyanne and Kim. That was even more heart-breaking. I needed to borrow her crayons. I knew exactly how she felt—wrenched from her roots. I was now having to deal for the second time with what she was feeling, but, luckily, she was young enough to forget. When we have spoken of that experience, she has assured me, "I don't even remember it, Mum, I realise it was so much harder on you."

Just one of the many heart-breaking pictures that Helen drew.

I took little interest in the "Welcome to Your New Home" cards that began arriving, except for one from John's mother, the message of which briefly perked my interest, "You know what they say? New home, new baby!" Some chance of that! But I must have started talking to John again sooner than I remember, because baby Nicola arrived on the scene within the year. I had softened my stance and acquiesced to one of Mahatma Gandhi's famous quotes, applying it to my own situation, "When the power of love overcomes the love of power there will be peace."

CHAPTER THIRTEEN

Still round the corner, there may wait a new road or a secret gate.

— J.R.R Tolkien

Our cabin in the woods—Lions Bay 1972

I LIKE TO CALL the next phase of our life our pioneer period in the boonies. Many people had not even heard of Lions Bay. The Upper Levels Highway was still under construction, and our mail was collected from boxes eight miles down the road. We had basically taken up residence in the bush, clinging precariously to the side of a mountain. The house was a wooden cabin—albeit a nice one with an en-suite bathroom—hidden away in far too many tall trees in the middle of a rock pile. The wild animals were not easily going to relinquish their territory, and why should they? Bears, raccoons and skunks wandered at will around the house. Packs of coyotes howled in the woods at night. We were warned to watch for cougars that had occasionally been known to carry off small children in other rural areas. Those residents who were already living in the old established part of Lions Bay may question the accuracy of my description, but that new part of Lions Bay had only just had the road bulldozed through and building lots configured.

There were only two other houses on the street at the time, but one of them wasn't exactly a house—it was a masterpiece—a

Just a little handyman special.

work of art—hewn from lumber, rock, and the blood sweat and tears of the new occupants.

We were dumbfounded when we learned that the owners, Harold, a logger, and Flo Gienger had built and furnished the whole thing unaided. In Wales, it was normal practice to hire a builder—most of the men there were considered ingenious if they had built book shelves or a compost box. The two-storey house that we had just moved into—I was far from ready to call it my house—would have fitted nicely into the living room, and we could have parked the car in the fireplace. As a matter of fact, we could have burned the car in the fireplace because by that time the body of our Datsun was 85% plastic wood. The height of the living room was enough for a 25-30-ft-tall Christmas tree, rivalling the one in Trafalgar Square.

We would be amazed when we saw the tree that first Christmas. Only a logger would have had the necessary skills to

Will it go through the back door?

hew it down. John, along with other people who were collared as they were driving by, were asked to help haul it into the house.

It would take the whole family, and possibly one of the older sons acting as a trapeze artist swinging from the chandelier, to manoeuvre it into position, and it would take several days to decorate it.

This smaller tree may have been only 25ft tall—chandelier in the foreground.

Meanwhile, not knowing much about the habits of the evergreens that grew around us, at that stage, we would choose a lacy looking, four-ft-tall tree which would drop all its needles three days after it had been decorated. That is how we would learn that hemlocks do not make suitable Christmas trees, and have to replace it with a sturdy fir.

In future years, Harold would cut trees for all the neighbours, but they would also be huge, so getting them into position and decorating them would result in some challenges for the recipients.

How many people does it take to put up the Enns's "free" Christmas tree?

Flo and Harold Gienger were both from Russian immigrant families who had escaped across Europe during the Revolution, so they had been brought up to be strong, independent, and intimidatingly accomplished. I was yet to meet them, but they had already introduced themselves to John who had temporarily ended his baptism of fire on a tug, and had since started working as a marine surveyor, so was able to re-adopt that air of the fine English gentleman from Henley-on-Thames. And what had they been thinking about me, one wonders—a woman who had been swanning around England and Wales with the children while her husband had been rushed off his feet trying his best to get her a home ready to move into on her return—a princess perhaps? These were not the kind of people who moved in those circles—they didn't suffer wimps gladly. John wondered if he should buy a pair of hobnailed boots, a couple of heavy ropes and a chain-saw to prove what he was really made of.

Long before Christmas, we met the young couple, Jon and Pam Strom, who lived in the other house below us. We had already been told that they had a stone fireplace which was sliding down the mountain without the house attached. "Come and sit around the fire," had a different connotation for their guests.

Pam, a Welsh girl, was very leery of meeting John when she heard he had been in the Merchant Marine.

She was right on side with Lady Astor. Pam had been a children's hostess on British passenger liners and had past experience of John's type. Being the only woman on the ship with officer status and beautiful into the bargain, I can just imagine how she must have spent her time fending off unwanted attention. For a while, she avoided us, but when she heard I was also Welsh and we shared the same birthday, she felt that John must be safe. It was still a relief, however, when she discovered that she had not met him on a ship previously.

Despite our initial cultural differences and difficulties with Canadian versus British terms we knew immediately that we would become the best of friends with those warm and welcoming neighbours. In the case of the Giengers, our terminology needed a few adjustments. When John began on the landscaping project and told Harold that he was exhausted from humping rocks and that I was just putting a joint in the oven, we noticed that Harold began to keep his distance. On entering their house, one was always invited to "pull up a stump." Initially, people might have thought that they should have arrived with some heavy equipment, but those "stumps" were seats that had been hewn in one piece from logs and could cause one a hernia with the effort it took to drag them out from the table. We have happy memories of sitting on those "stumps" at the enormous, polished burl dining table while Harold "bucked up" the roast, and eating Flo's Mum's "pie by the yard" at the kitchen bar. At our 50th year in Canada celebration, the girls wrote a skit entitled, "Fifty Reasons why we are glad that Mum and Dad moved to Canada." One of the reasons given was that they were happy to have been introduced to Grandma Fleming's "pie by the yard" rather than being subjected to a steady diet of spotted dick.

   Like Ineke, my Richmond neighbour, Flo was an immaculate housekeeper, although her house was one to be lived in. Her obsession was with bathing. Having grown up with the tin bath on the side of the house which was brought in occasionally, but never more than once a week, I was not so meticulous. She and her children would be in the bathtub at least once a day, and as ours were growing up they would have as many baths at the Gienger's house as at ours. If they went within three feet of the back door they would be scooped up, thrown in the bathtub with Flo's children and come home for dinner dressed in spotlessly clean pyjamas. Flo had grown up in a religious home which had not really rubbed off on her, but she clearly believed that "cleanliness is next to godliness."

   Eventually, I would tell Flo the true story of the house purchase and how hopping mad I had been with John, but my anger paled in comparison to Flo's. She seemed to spend half her life being furious with her husband. She told me that she got so mad with him that she could "piss up a rope." I believe such an action defies the law of gravity, but I have never witnessed it. At other times, she was "madder than a wet hen." I have never been a witness to the habits of wet hens either, even though I had lived all my young life on a farm in Wales. In the first few years, power cuts were a common occurrence, as wind storms brought trees crashing down on the power lines. Lions Bay had no street lights anyway, so it was always "as dark as the inside of a cow," to quote Flo, but one has to assume that she couldn't prove it although she came from the dairy farming area of Chilliwack.

   John had taken a sizeable cut in salary to become a marine surveyor so with the increase of $4,000 on our mortgage to $21,000 we were skint, or, as my grandmother had said of the penurious state of our old neighbours in Wales, the Johnsons, "We didn't have a pot to piss in."

   I will never forget the night that the Giengers came over with a bottle of wine to drink with us. We had broken all but three of the glasses from the abominable "Three Room Group," so what to do? Well, John could have pretended that he was not going to have a drink, or invented some other plausible story, but he has always enjoyed embarrassing me. To my horror, he came in from the kitchen having poured the wine into the three glasses and a china bowl that he then proceeded to overtly drink from himself, as if this was common practice. When I reminded him of this incident recently, he roared with laughter and claimed he had no memory of it. Fortunately, the neighbours are polite enough to pretend that they don't remember it either.

We weren't in a position to buy more glasses for some time, but as luck would have it, free glasses were being given out with a $3.00 fill-up. We had to drive the Datsun until it was literally running on fumes to get in the $3.00 worth of gas to qualify, but in that way, we built up a motley collection of glasses which were as hideous as those remaining from the unsightly "Three Room Group."

There was one other house on a street nearby into which a young Danish couple, Ted and Riggi, had moved. Ted owned a bakery and was affectionately known as "Ted the Bread." They had two girls and were expecting a third. Jon and Pam had a little boy—Jordan, and were expecting a second, Flo and Harold had a two-month-old daughter, Tanya, and a son of eighteen months, Troy, as well as two older boys, Travis and Shawn, from Flo's previous marriage—her first husband, the father of the two boys, had been killed, at the age of 24, in a crash of one of the Star Fighters in France when the older boy was just a year, and she was pregnant with the second. Travis and Shawn were very well brought up—at the age of 61, Travis still insists on calling us Mr. and Mrs. Dudley—and they were great baby-sitters although Travis didn't last as long as Shawn. He had a secret cabin to build deep in the forest with his old school friends. We are eternally grateful that he managed to persuade one of them, Robert, to buy our almost wooden car.

Before long, houses started appearing like mushrooms on the street, and soon they were filled with young families with children, so we became, once more, a part of a real neighbourhood. Helen joined the Lions Bay preschool, and finally stopped drawing pictures of her old friends.

John's life as a marine surveyor was unfortunately very short-lived. A lengthy longshoreman's strike almost decimated the business, and as the writing was on the wall, John asked the boss if it would help him out if he returned to sea. The boss was relieved, and John agreed to work for him occasionally on his weeks off when the strike was over which suited everyone and gave us a much-needed boost to our income.

That summer, my mother came for a visit. It was unfortunate, but not surprising, that she had timed it to leave only two days before her third grandchild was due. My mother was not the easiest of guests to please. She was completely dependent on me for entertainment and the day before she left, in desperation, I took her for a stroll in Lighthouse Park. I could hardly walk with the weight of the baby bearing down, but I struggled along until we arrived at the lighthouse. I was sure she would be impressed with the view, but her only comment was. "When you've seen one lighthouse, you've seen 'em all." My mother had never ceased to surprise me.

John had returned to sea, and I was at the beach with the girls when I went into labour, so had to get home, feed the children and get to the hospital as quickly as possible. Unfortunately, neither of my friends, Flo or Barb, who were slated to drive me there were in the village, but after a few frantic calls, I located another neighbour whose husband cared for Helen and Alison while she drove me to St. Vincent's hospital. My doctor was then living on Eagle Island which required a short boat trip, so it was touch and go if either of us would make it in time. It was 7.30 p.m. when we got into the elevator to the maternity ward and Nicola arrived at 8.16 p.m. Flo and Barb were stunned that it was all over by the time they came home.

The doctor had told me that he didn't like to have husbands in the delivery room. Well, there was no fear of that. Mine was towing a log barge around Cape Scott at the north end of Vancouver Island and didn't turn up for three days. I felt like an unwed mother. Without my husband, and separated from my other two girls, what should have been such a pivotal moment in my life was such a let-down. I kept assuring the other women in the ward that my husband would be coming soon, but they looked increasingly sceptical as days went by.

John's painting of the tug he was on when his third daughter was born.

I had called the office to ask if someone there could radio to let John know the baby had arrived. When he was told, "John you have a beautiful baby daughter," he replied, "You've got to be kidding!" He laughs when he remembers that statement, knowing how proud he is of his three girls and how he wouldn't change anything for the world.

Now our family was complete.

CHAPTER FOURTEEN

Living through a home renovation is like living in the wild. You do whatever it takes to survive.

— Author unknown

HAVING BUILT A SANDPIT and a two-storey play-house in the garden for the children, John believed he had the necessary experience to finish the basement. If other men could build houses, he was confident that completing just the lower floor would be a piece of cake. While he has always been hardworking and motivated, accuracy has never been his strong point or anything he believed was important. To be fair, he had to overcome some serious inaccuracies that were already built in. The basement floor sloped badly downhill—although it wasn't in immediate danger of joining Pam and Jon's fireplace—and the walls weren't true. He began by installing the studs and thought it would be a cinch, much like having a new baby to care for.

He made excellent progress until he got to the last stud in what would become the downstairs bathroom. No matter how hard he tried to position it, there was resistance—but nothing, apparently, that could not be fixed with a bit of brute force and a sledge hammer. Feeling a sense of accomplishment as the last stud slotted into place, he called me down to admire his workmanship. "Hang on, I'm in the bathroom," I called before flushing the toilet. I heard a scream from below and rushed down to find him looking like a drowned rat covered in bits of toilet paper and detritus and standing in a pool of sewage. The force had caused the longer stud to remove the upstairs toilet right off its base. He took a shower, while I called the plumber.

That didn't slow down Mr. Fix-it. Very soon after that, there seemed to be some kind of blockage in one of the toilets, and John's solution was to locate the pipe leading into the septic tank and stick the hose up it with the water on full force. That appeared to do the trick, but what a sight met our eyes when we went into the upstairs bathrooms. The blockage was cleared alright, but there were stalactites of shit hanging from the ceilings and the walls. The smell was suffocating. We spent several days cleaning up the mess. To provide more warmth, we had recently installed the left-over white shag carpet in the bathrooms. Our stupidity held no bounds.

John wasn't deterred, however, and he did, in fact, finish the job, including a floor-to-ceiling, rock fireplace. All fireplaces in the seventies were made from local rock—they had replaced the fake teak feature walls of the sixties, and most of them, including ours, were hideous. The finishing touch was orange shag carpet throughout—another wonderful designer feature of the times that came with a free rake. It became so popular that people even covered up their beautiful solid oak and maple floors with it. John got really carried away with using the left-over pieces; he covered the children's toy box, carpeted the attic floor of their playhouse, and anything else that was easily coverable was covered. It was a true orange bonanza!

He had built a beautiful deck around the house earlier on which had taken up a lot of the driveway, so when he had finished the interior renovations, he embarked on a project that would give us extra parking space. By building a high wall on the steep slope to the right side of the house, he believed he could make a flat space for at least two cars. There were rocks galore on the property and he had seen enough of those dry stone walls in Britain that had been there for centuries.

He knew that his wall would need to be at least 14-ft-high, and being a fast worker, he had constructed it in no time. With all the homes being built in the area, fill was readily available, so he invited builders to deposit any trucks full of rocks and dirt into the hole. In no time at all, the area was flat and set off the house nicely.

A few weeks later after very heavy rains, we heard an ominous crashing noise in the middle of the night. We thought it was an earthquake, but in the morning, we discovered half the wall was missing having disappeared down the slope along with lots of extra rocks that had been gifted by builders. So how did those ancient peoples do it?

Living as we did in the boonies, we depended so much on our neighbours for help in rough times. Once John had purchased the chain-saw—and I need to be accurate here, because he didn't buy his own until he had wrecked several of the neighbour's—he thought we should buy a wood-stove to save on our heating bills. There was an abundance of wood around us, not to mention the never-ending free supply salvaged from old barges at Island Tug. Besides that, aren't wood stoves an essential part of the boonies lifestyle?

Explaining the release valve which didn't, and blew through the ceiling.

This was a wood boiler that linked up to the hot water system and right from the beginning was destined to end in disaster. It had always scared me stiff, so on the morning I woke to ominous knocking sounds in the pipes, I grabbed the kids from their beds, clutched the cat under my arm—there wasn't time to collect the photo albums—and raced over to the neighbours screaming that the house was going to blow up.

While we all shivered in our night-clothes on the lawn, Harold took his life in his hands by entering the house to see what could be done. By that time, the pressure had blown the valve off the top of the boiler, and water and smoke were filling the basement. The orange shag was soaked, and it appeared to be payback time for the poor man who had purchased our Richmond home. This time, I called the plumber as well as a water and fire restoration crew.

Not long after that, John was able to reciprocate Harold's brave gesture by coming to Flo's rescue. She called from her bed in the early hours of the morning to report that a flying squirrel had got caught up in her hair. By the time John arrived, the squirrel had extricated itself and flown up to the rafters, 20 feet above the bed—well out of reach of the broom that John had brought along to solve the problem. If you were in any doubt before, you must now have concluded that we were indeed living in the boonies.

CHAPTER FIFTEEN

Don't ever question the value of volunteerism. Noah's Ark was built by volunteers, the Titanic was built by professionals.

Submitted by Dave Gynn Coleman

IN THE VILLAGE AT that time, we were fortunate to have a wonderful handy-man called Frank—a Jack of all trades who looked after the needs of the village which were far less in those days before the population grew and bureaucracy was forced upon us from external quarters. Whatever the problem, we called Frank. He didn't just look after all the village maintenance issues all year long and plough the roads in the winter, he cared for all of us. If a car wouldn't start or someone drove his or hers into a ditch or over the side of an impossibly steep driveway—a fairly common occurrence—we called Frank. He rescued cats stuck in trees, shooed away bears from gardens, captured baby skunks trapped in garbage cans and came to the rescue of people who might have stepped out onto their balcony and accidentally locked themselves out of their home. When someone new to the neighbourhood had a problem, we would automatically say, "Call Frank." Every neighbourhood needed a Frank. He had the Lions Bay Works' shed named after him—God rest his soul.

This, of course, meant that volunteerism became part and parcel of living in a small community. The year before we had moved in, Lions Bay had been incorporated as a village, so we then acquired a Mayor and Council.

The first Mayor was Curly Stewart whose great grandfather had fought in the Crimean War. Such ancestry must have been quite an asset when parrying the onslaught of criticism which is about all the thanks one ever gets when running for public office.

A very old fire engine had been purchased so that had to be manned. Then a Search and Rescue group was formed, followed by an Ambulance Service. John joined the Fire Department along with a few ladies who were around in the daytime and, later on, I became a member of the Ambulance Service.

Now that we have a highly trained, professional group of fire-fighters and paramedics serving in all those capacities, I think back to the days when none of us had the skills or proper training to deal with the emergencies, or the serious accidents that occurred on our winding, mountain road. I sometimes wonder if we did more harm than good.

I well remember how nervous I was on my first call-out. My partner, Don, had asked me to be the attendant because, he explained, he couldn't see. That didn't bode well for a man who was about to drive an ambulance to an accident site at high speed with sirens blaring. The call-out was for a man who had collapsed chopping wood along the highway. I was panicking—what was I going to do when I reached him? Would I remember the ABCs? Could I tell if he was breathing? Would I be able to determine if he had a pulse? Would I have forgotten how to administer CPR? Phew! I am embarrassed to say that it was a huge relief to discover that he was already dead, and that there was nothing for me to do but tell Don to call the coroner.

With Don at the wheel, that ambulance got quite banged up. One unforgettable day, we had driven on to the ferry to collect a woman having a miscarriage, and as we drove off, we managed to sheer off all the lights and sirens from the top of the ambulance. I looked through the back window to see the doctor who had been attending the woman before the "experts" arrived shaking his head in disbelief.

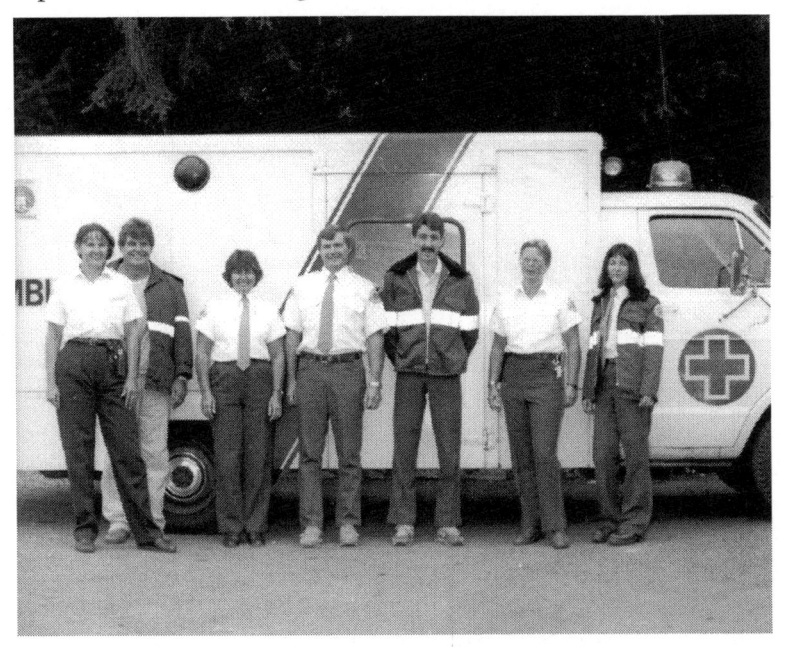

The crew cleverly disguising the dings on the ambulance.

Because John had so much time off, he would occasionally be called to drive the ambulance. One day—it was his birthday—he was summoned to pick up a man with a back injury. Once the man was stabilised and comfortable, John took off with sirens blaring and lights flashing. He had neither learned about the code system—that lights and sirens were only necessary for real emergencies—nor that back injuries have to be transported with care.

As he raced along well above the speed limit, with cars moving out of his way, a sudden feeling of power overcame him, and he arrived at the hospital having driven along the Upper Levels Highway and down the middle of Lonsdale Avenue through every red light at breakneck speed. As the patient was being taken into the hospital, a nurse came out and said, "For God's sake why don't you turn off that bloody siren?" That, however, was not enough to burst his bubble. He was still experiencing an adrenalin rush and declared it the best birthday present he had ever had. I'm guessing that he returned home with that "bloody siren" still wailing.

He thinks back to his experiences in the Fire Department and recalls one call-out that ended reasonably well, but could have been serious. The fire-engine at the time, was very old and didn't have synchronised gears which meant one had to double de-clutch to get it into gear. On a call to a chimney fire along the highway, John failed to get the truck into gear so crawled along the highway at 15 m.p.h. with the traffic building up behind him and impatient drivers blasting their horns. It took so long to reach the house that the fire was already out, but to be sure, John decided to clean out the chimney by getting up on the roof and lowering a garden rake tied to a piece of string. The rope suddenly went slack so John, who had obviously not been paying attention in basic Science classes at school and hadn't learned that string and fire are not compatible, yelled down to one of the crew in the room below, "Has the rake come through yet?" receiving the response, "Not yet." John keeps meaning to tell the new owners that they don't need to buy a new rake because they already own one, stored away in a very safe place.

Living as we do surrounded by forest, the thought of a devastating fire is never far from anyone's mind. We know from observing blackened trees above us that fires have raged through in the past, so it is only a matter of time.

During the 1980s after a particularly hot summer, slash burning was underway in Cypress Park, on the other side of the mountain from Lions Bay, when the wind came up causing the fire to burn out of control. Before long, it was spreading over the ridge, trees were bursting into flames and the wind gathered strength producing giant fireballs which ignited small fires all over the mountain above us.

The firemen were told to begin advising residents to evacuate the village and when John got word to me, I packed the children, the cat and all the photo albums into the car ready to escape. The owner of an isolated house further down the highway called the firehall to report that his house was surrounded by fire, but when the fire-truck arrived on site, it was obvious that the amount of available water was not sufficient to be of much use, so the owner was told to evacuate. It looked like a hopeless situation.

As the firemen were returning to the village, the first drops of rain began to fall, and by the time they were back at base, the rain was torrential. I don't think many of the villagers were aware how close they had come to losing their homes that night. Someone was looking out for us. With global warming bringing increasingly hot summers, we can only hope that someone will continue to look out for us.

Those were events that are only amusing talking points now, but Lions Bay and the surrounding communities have seen their share of tragedy with loss of life caused by overflowing creeks, falling boulders, a devastating house fire which killed two small children, and an unsafe highway where head-on collisions were common. The volunteer firemen and the ambulance crews have had to deal with situations that give them nightmares to this day, and back then there were no counsellors at hand to mitigate their trauma.

We lived through some horrendous times as debris torrents roared down the creeks. Harvey Creek was the first to go causing heavy flooding and bank erosion which left one house hanging precariously over space.

Pat Carney who lived in Lions Bay and became an MP in 1980, and would later be appointed to the Canadian Senate, had written an article about Harvey Creek in May 1968 expressing her concern about the logging practices which had been going on above our village. Perhaps, if someone in government had taken her seriously and acted on her warnings, many of the tragedies could have been avoided.

The first disaster causing death was when the old wooden bridge over M Creek was washed out in a slide and people, not realising that the bridge had been destroyed, drove straight into the chasm with the loss of nine lives. Less than two months later, a similar situation at Strachan Creek resulted in the death of a pregnant woman who was washed over a bridge into

Howe Sound, and in 1983 the same happened on Alberta Creek in Lions Bay burying two teenage brothers under four to six feet of mud.

Alberta Creek was once a small, insignificant stream, so no one could have imagined the devastation that resulted from the avalanche of mud, rocks, stumps and water that was unleashed from high up the mountainside on that fateful night—February 11th, 1983.

We were living on Bayview Rd., 150 m away from the creek, but in the early hours of the morning, as our house shook and the ground vibrated, we assumed we were experiencing an earthquake. As the wall of debris swept down from above, every bridge was reduced to rubble, power poles and lines were downed, the transformers all blew with deafening explosions, and flashes that lit up the sky, and there followed an eerie silence. We were terrified, but had no idea what had occurred until John, who was a member of the fire department, was called out. Then, it didn't take long for us to learn about the immensity of the tragedy that had befallen the village.

News reached the firemen that two boys were trapped in a small trailer on the far side of the creek, but as the firemen were going to rescue them, they heard what sounded like express trains as additional slides of mud and debris rumbled down the creek. Then, believing that the worst was over, some of the men roped themselves together to cross to the other side to reach the boys. They had just made it to the far bank when another plug of mud, boulders the size of cars, stumps and whole trees roared by, sweeping the creek bed clean.

The trailer in which the boys, Tom and David Wade, had been sleeping was crushed beyond recognition and the home in which they had lived with their parents and sisters was knocked off its foundations. Fortunately, the firemen were able to rescue the boys' sister who was trapped in the basement but miraculously unhurt.

The next few days were a blur as everyone tried to come to terms with the Wade family's loss. Three other homes had been totally destroyed, others damaged, and back yards washed into the ocean. As well as the main highway bridge, six crossings in the village had been destroyed, cutting off one quarter of the community.

Reflecting on that time now—considering the extent of the tragedy—I realise how quickly things came together and how many people worked such long hours and so efficiently to make it happen. I don't think any of us knew how much we owed to Doug Pollock, the Mayor at the time, who with the council members, had to make so many snap decisions while trying to negotiate with the various levels of government as well as the ever-present press. Power, water and phone service was rapidly restored, and a temporary bridge was in operation on Bayview Road within two days. The firemen who were already exhausted, physically and mentally, continued to keep a 24-hour vigil, and the village hall became a canteen serving a continuous supply of sandwiches and soup for all the workers and volunteers. It was Lions Bay at its worst and its finest!

We all have ingrained memories of that dreadful time, but I will forever have an image of a church filled to capacity with an entire village in mourning, while two white caskets holding young men robbed of a future, were borne in by teenage friends too young for a sadness they will continue to carry around for the rest of their lives.

John and I were attending a Lions Bay school staff party in Strachan Creek, a community just down the highway, when we witnessed that earlier disaster. The creek began to show early signs of a mud slide which posed a risk to the community, so we had to be evacuated. A German student who had just flown in that day was isolated in a house nearby. The owners were unable to get back along the highway so called our hosts asking for the young man to be made aware of the danger. John and another guest went over to the house in the darkness, where what appeared to be a large area of blacktop turned out to be a deep pond into which John plunged in over his head. He thought it was game over—that he'd had his chips. As he dragged himself out, he was able to borrow clothes from his host, Ken, and seemed none the worse for his near-drowning experience.

A ferry was sent out to rescue us, but the wind was so strong that one of its Zodiacs could not make it close enough to the shore. Next, a train was sent along the tracks, but a falling tree prevented us from getting far. Finally, a bus was sent to our rescue, and we were able to scramble up the steep bank to get to the highway. By that time, the media had been alerted, so we were all filmed on the bus carrying the desserts and bottles and glasses of wine that we had been determined not to forfeit. It was embarrassing to be called the next day by so many people who had seen we revellers on the news. We had no idea that night, that the pregnant woman had drowned.

Returning by water taxi next day, I was met by a resident, Dave Butler, on the beach who lamented, "The whole village has been destroyed." It was, indeed, a scene of devastation, with at least 500 trees uprooted and power poles and lines down everywhere. Two houses had been flattened by falling trees. There were three trees down on our property. Fortunately, our babysitter, Michael Enns, had put our children and himself safely under the bed.

The road was closed for many days following that disaster and since John was on shift he remained on the other side. Our only way out if there had been an emergency would have been to travel north or call for a water taxi.

John was ecstatic about the new supply of free wood from the downed trees, and once he could get home, he lost no time in getting out into the forest, almost killing himself in the process. He had bought an old Husqvarna saw from Harold so began to fancy himself as an experienced logger. He went to work in an area where trees were all crisscrossing each other, and when standing on one, while cutting through another above his head—something only a neophyte would do—he heard a deafening crack, as both ends of the sawn tree flew up into the air. He was thrown on his back and watched the saw spiral into the sky and disappear. While he lay there winded, he could hear it still ticking away about 100 ft into the bush.

Not deterred, however, he spent days collecting and stacking logs on our lower deck, which was attached to the house on one side, but on 12-ft posts on the lower side. He was thrilled when he had chopped and arranged two 30-ft rows in place— "our whole winter's supply," he thought, giving himself a well-deserved pat on the back. He stepped back to admire his work and there was a deafening roar as the deck detached itself from the house and pitched itself and all the wood twenty feet down the bank. It was a challenging winter climbing down to retrieve the wood, piece by piece, to feed the wood-stove.

Flo's father, Henry, would shake his head as he gazed at the mountains above us wondering what fools would choose to live on a mountainside that was so unstable, and along a highway that was so unsafe, but despite the risks, and with the exception of a couple of families who were scared away, everyone else hung in. Many of the dangers have since been mitigated with the building of catchment basins on the creeks, wooden bridges replaced with concrete ones and, thanks to the 2010 Winter Olympics, a four-lane divided highway. Those of us who have been here for years, as well as all the new-comers, believe that because of the camaraderie, and the small village atmosphere, there is no better place on earth to live.

I think back to those early days with nostalgia. Everyone worked hard—hewing wood, building decks and landscaping properties. I was no princess—I can tell you—I could hump rocks with the best of them. We wrestled with our rock pile and conquered it in record time, even managing to create a sizeable lawn which fifty years on nature has reclaimed. With the rate of growth in our rainforest, I believe that if we all moved away for five years, we would have to fight our way back in, much like the prince who had to battle his way through a thicket of thorns and vines to rescue Sleeping Beauty.

We found cedar saplings in the forest to make a hedge around the property—a hedge that would grow tall enough in very few years to block the view and cause great angst and expense to the home-owners who moved in above us. In fact, small trees that so many people planted in the old days continue to be the primary cause of conflict to this day. Some of those trees have grown as much as 80-100 ft since we came to Lions Bay in 1972 and have obliterated views and engulfed homes. Those who still refuse to remove a tree to restore a neighbour's view or let in light don't seem to appreciate the pace of deterioration that occurs in wooden homes surrounded by tall trees, and how the lack of sun can, according to research, seriously affect the psyche.

Apart from the view-blocking cedars, we planted a small fir hedge between our property and the neighbours' which has grown into a row of massive trees at least 50ft in height.

CHAPTER SIXTEEN

You can't expect to be old and wise if you were never young and crazy.

— Author Unknown

THOSE EARLY YEARS WERE what I might refer to as our wilder years. After our house was completed, our builder constructed an architect designed home for our neighbours, a young advertising executive, David Enns, and his wife Barb. It had an enormous deck and became the perfect party house. When we hadn't all pulled up our "stumps" around the neighbours' bar or weren't kicking up our heels, hooting and hollering at events in the village hall, the sound of Neil Diamond, Roberta Flack, John Denver, and Olivia Newton John could be regularly heard blaring forth from their house competing with the howling coyotes.

We formed a gourmet dinner club which then led to progressive dinners that started at 5 p.m. and went on for hours. John recalls one where he partook of the canapés and champagne before leaving for the office at 5.30 p.m. and returned after a twelve-hour-shift to join us for dessert and Spanish coffee at 6:30 a.m. next day.

Are we having fun yet? Barb and Dave at a gourmet dinner.

 The pig roasts at Furry Creek were legendary, as were the midnight dips at the beach and a midnight swim in a polluted lake in Abbotsford which was probably the cause of some nasty boils that I had to have lanced at the hospital and the reason that it was just a one-time event. We all owe it to Flo who stood on the shore, disgusted by our behaviour but holding clean towels for all of us. Flo had always been the one in full control—someone had to be.

 One of our more sober activities was hymn-singing evenings around the piano. I hope someone will volunteer to sing "The Old Rugged Cross" at my funeral for old times' sake, and if Harold outlives me perhaps he will dust off his trumpet which, as a young man, he had played in the Salvation Army band.

 Involving the women only, there were lunches at Pat Wade's that lasted late into the evening. She was another of those born hostesses—only she could have organised a surprise birthday party for her friend, Rosalind, at 5.30 a.m. which lasted until 6 p.m. when she had to recruit Rosalind's husband to drive home her inebriated guests, including my mother-in-law.

Pat—centre—loved to hold parties, but she could never get people to leave.

Most memorable for me on the wildness scale were two trips we took to the Medieval Inn. Prior to those, we had hired a bus to take us to a dance hall across the border so someone had the bright idea that we could do that without travelling so far—most likely John of driving aversion.

The Medieval Inn had been the brainchild of two British ex-pats who introduced a British spin of the past onto the Vancouver dining scene. The restaurant was set up with décor befitting the times, and patrons were expected to behave like drunken peasants. Our group needed not a tad of encouragement. On arrival, everyone was plied with copious mugs of cheap mead by the "wenches" to ensure the evening went off to a successful start. Well before any food arrived on the scene, every person was three sheets to the wind with no effort on his or her part.

Those present on that first night will still have a vision of John not behaving at all like the refined English gentleman that they had believed him to be. They will remember him singing raunchy rugby songs with such a look of innocence on his face, and then dancing on the table with one of the neighbours, Jackie—wife of the blind ambulance driver—and sharing a suit of armour—part of the décor which they had seen fit to take apart.

Who would have thought, at the time, that this was a man who would become a pillar of society, a Citizen of the Year, a man who would support the downtrodden in Vancouver, the Indigenous people of Guatemala and Peru and several Syrian refugee families? Who would have believed that he would dedicate his life to building and maintaining trails for the benefit of everyone in his own neighbourhood, winning a prestigious award for so doing in the name of a selfless leader of the North Shore Rescue team? Who would have thought he would become a green-tea drinking vegetarian? Certainly not anyone who was witness to his behaviour that night. But, as they say, life is full of surprises.

And what of the guest who shall remain nameless who, on the second visit was exiting the restaurant unable to bear to sacrifice all those bowls of fruit left on the tables that she felt she had paid for. She had obviously not recovered from memories of childhood deprivation so despite opposition, she collected pounds of fruit and deposited them into her skirt. Heavy fruit in a skirt of a wrap-around style didn't bode well and soon the inevitable happened. The fruit rolled out onto the street and into the gutters to the surprise of all those passers-by and the homeless people sleeping in doorways. Not to be deterred, she gathered it all up and instead of thinking it might be a nice gesture to hand it around to the needy, she laid out her skirt on the sidewalk, scooped up the fruit, threw the heavy skirt over her shoulder and marched back to the bus with her loot, quite unperturbed that she was sitting there in her underwear. Childhood deprivation can lead people to behave in strange ways.

It was in the early hours of the morning that the group arrived back in Lions Bay, but instead of going home which is what most decent people would have done, they decided to party on, and those who could still walk staggered up the hill. The lady loaded down with fruit was unable to walk at that stage and was feeling the effects of too much cheap mead, so she had to be carried. Who should come along doing his early rounds? None other than Frank! He looked at the drunken mob but acted as if this was completely normal behaviour. "Good morning everyone," he said, cheerfully, and went on his way. Good old Frank!—we knew he would be discreet.

It was unfortunate for the lady who had to be carried that her desire to continue to enjoy the night which was rapidly morphing into daylight was cut short by a spinning head. She was soon on her knees clinging to the toilet bowl, feeling like death, while a dutiful and understanding husband stood by her side flushing the toilet each time she vomited. She, it was hoped, had learned a hard lesson. He may have been reminded of another time the lady had over-imbibed, and he had gallantly dug holes on a Spanish beach.

It was following that first visit to the Medieval Inn that John gave up drinking for good, and the rest of us probably should have followed his example. The Gienger's daughter, Tanya, and our children who have moved back to the village say that they remember us having so much more fun than they have now, but despite the terrible example we set, they are far more sensible and responsible than we were and much more protective of their children. I believe it may be something to do with the fact that we were really pioneers who had to work so hard against impossible odds, or maybe it was because, unlike we, who were all in our late twenties or early thirties, they had their children much later in life and were already long past our level of energy and exuberance. Maybe, I am just making excuses for our crazy behaviour. But, as the saying goes, we are all much older and wiser now not to mention too knackered to stay awake much beyond 9.00 p.m.

As I write, we are in the fourteenth month of the Covid-19 pandemic, and I have just read about an idea that our neighbour, Peter, has pitched—a rocking, all-night party to celebrate the end of it. I will be at least eighty-years-old by then, but I have promised him that we will all do our level best to re-live those heady days of the early seventies.

So, although my introduction to my new home in Lions Bay had not been a happy event and had caused more than a little marital tension, because of the welcoming neighbours and the small village atmosphere, I obviously warmed to the house and the neighbourhood. I have tried to recall exactly when I truly felt that I belonged, and it had to be the day that I had returned home from a hard day at Collingwood School where I had been teaching for a few years. I was relaxing in the bathtub, unwinding with a glass of sherry, when a whole group of children burst into the bathroom. As they stood around the bathtub all talking at once while I tried to determine what was so urgent, one child was staring at me in fascination. She said, "My Mum has those, she calls 'em tits," I didn't think the neighbourhood could get much more intimate than that.

CHAPTER SEVENTEEN

A one-room school is not just about education. It builds pride in the community.

— Mark De Watt

LIONS BAY SCHOOL WASN'T built when we first arrived. Prior to its opening, the children were bussed to a larger school in Horseshoe Bay. It opened after Easter of 1979, too late for Helen, but in time for Alison to finish her Kindergarten year. The parents who presently have their children in attendance would be mystified to learn about the nasty battles that went on between the parents who were delighted by the prospect of a small neighbourhood school and a group who fought tooth and nail to prevent it. Those who balked at the idea felt that their children would be disadvantaged by being in such a limited environment and would miss out on opportunities that would arise from mixing with children in a larger setting. These were the same parents who had chosen to live in a small rural community for its obvious benefits. It made no sense to those of us who wanted the same experience for our children.

It was an unfortunate time for our normally harmonious village because it pitted friends against friends and ended up being a game of winners and losers. Once the school was built despite the opposition, the parents who felt they had lost the battle were determined to make the lives of the teachers who were first employed unbearable. They were constantly at the school complaining and making demands, and even taking turns to sit in the school to observe and report to the School Board on anything that didn't fit with their idea of a sound education. As a teacher, I was quite used to dealing with parents who felt that they were qualified to judge because they had once gone to school themselves.

In a conversation I recently had with the librarian, Kathy, we agreed that the odd thing about that unfortunate period was that all those parents who behaved so unreasonably were such nice, sensible people who one would choose to have as friends. We concluded that one can't ever blame parents for wanting what they feel is best for their sons and daughters, no matter how misguided others may feel they are acting. Despite their fears that their children would "miss out", many of those children have brought honour to their community and have written glowing reports about what they see as the advantages of their early education in a rural school.

The school was architect designed and looked more like a clubhouse than a school, so there were some initial problems. The Kindergarten classroom was open-plan on the second floor and the noise that was generated made it impossible for the teachers to cope in the area below which was just one huge open classroom. At great expense as well as the initial objections of the architect, there was no alternative but to close off the upstairs area with a glass wall.

Of course, the opening of the school resulted in a new wave of enthusiastic volunteerism. A first Parent Teacher Association was formed, of which Brenda, a future Mayor, became the chairperson. John also became a member of the PTA, and he soon organised a group of parents to landscape the grounds and then build a magnificent wooden playscape which served the children for many years without anyone getting seriously injured or killed. Despite that, playscapes these days have to be built to certain rigid standards and don't exactly encourage creative play. The children at Lions Bay school, however, are fortunate to have their imaginations stretched in a school set in nature with a stream running through and mud, rocks and sticks galore at their disposal.

The original playscape built by John and his crew. The main beams were cut from the forest.

Today's parents are still enthusiastic volunteers and seem to put in even more time and energy than my generation. They provide hot meals, run after-school programmes, and are supportive of the staff. One parent even set up a garden where the students grow vegetables that they sell to provide funds for the school. In Wales, I and many others of my generation had that experience in our village schools over 75 years ago, so it is rewarding to see the return of such initiatives.

I feel very privileged to have seen my children and grandchildren attend the same school which is rare nowadays but was common in times past. It gives one such a feeling of permanence. If only I can persuade the grandchildren, when they grow up, to return home and continue the tradition.

It is sad that our children were really the last generation to experience real freedom and lives unhampered by over-protective parents and the bombardment of technology. They played outdoors all day long and were rarely seen except when they were called for meals. They invented games, sorted out their differences, rode their bikes on the street, walked to their friends' homes, to the bus and school and to the few activities that were available in the village hall with little parent involvement. Nowadays, children seem to spend half their lives being taxied around in SUVs by stressed out parents, having what are called "play-dates" prearranged for them, or being hustled off to organised activities, the majority of which they will never pursue in their adult lives. Perhaps, we did our children a disservice by not driving them to soccer, hockey or tennis practises or ballet and music classes when they were young—they may have been appearing at Wimbledon, or become famous hockey stars or concert pianists by now. Maybe, we should not have been content to just let them amble slowly home from school to watch innocent programs like Sesame Street and Mr. Rogers before sitting down to a family dinner together to talk about their day, instead of grabbing snacks on the run between activities which seems to be more the rule than the exception nowadays. I hope there are still some parents out there who recognise the importance of family meal-times.

We didn't worry so much about our children, although, in retrospect, perhaps we should have been a tad more vigilant. As little ones, they scrambled down the banks to play in the creek and roamed through the forest to build forts where they could easily have encountered bears, coyotes and cougars.

Only recently, the children told us of a story that sent shivers up my spine. John had not realised that a rope ladder he had made for them to climb up had been hung close enough to the telephone and power lines for them to leap across to swing on. "Ted the Bread" and his wife, Riggi, would have been horrified if they had known that their three daughters, who they assumed were safely playing in our basement or in the playhouse, were the most agile of the children and were frequently in danger of being electrocuted. I remember an occasion when Nicola, at age four, loosened all her front teeth falling off her bike while racing the other children down the hills. We called our neighbour, Jon of sliding fireplace fame, and he, a dentist, pushed them all back into position and Nicola was back on her bike, racing down the hill the next day.

CHAPTER EIGHTEEN

And good neighbours make a huge difference in the quality of life—I agree

— Robert Fulghum

FORTY-NINE YEARS ON we are still here in Lions Bay. There was a brief spell when we moved into West Vancouver, but it wasn't planned. Having decided to build a new house, we had bought a plot of land ready for the construction. After the house sold, we were unable to find a rental one in Lions Bay while we were building which is why we had to look further afield.

One of the reasons for moving was that the house was showing signs of age which is what happens to wooden homes in a rainforest. We had come from a country where buildings stand for centuries, but our house was only eighteen-years-old and already deteriorating rapidly. The shake roof was beginning to rot from being in complete shade, and John had been flattening old food cans and shoving them between the shakes whenever a new leak appeared. By the time we left, the whole roof was glinting. Knowing the way his mind worked, I prayed that he wouldn't see that as a new business opportunity.

The day we moved into the rental house on Sentinel Hill, John walked to Dairy Queen in his bedroom slippers to buy ice-cream, was briefly enticed by the convenience and thought, "This big city living isn't such a bad idea," so we sold the lot that we had bought, planning to build a house in West Vancouver instead.

That lot was on the side of a creek and a year later, one third of it got washed away in a landslide. Fortunately, the purchaser had not yet built his home, so it was not the disaster it could have been. Later on, before we had committed to staying in West Vancouver, we bought another lot in Lions Bay that had a staggering view but which we were happy to sell because of its position on a busy corner and the number of ugly electrical and telephone wires on two sides that interrupted the view. Still being leery of electricity because I hadn't grown up with it in Wales, I managed to convince John that those heavy wires could also be a health hazard. He thought I was nuts, but being accustomed to my Welsh idiosyncrasies, he acquiesced to my wishes.

Although two of our children were already at University, the rental house became a hive of activity. It had a pool, so Nicola who was in her last year of high school became the most popular girl in her grade. Living so close to so many friends was a new experience for her because in Lions Bay she had been somewhat isolated. She certainly made the most of it. We felt some comfort that she, a new driver, would not be travelling along the dangerous highway because, being the third child, she tended to have a wilder streak.

She will remember one particular incident on New Year's Eve when she had planned to invite everyone over for a party at the house, knowing we were going out. She had talked her sister into buying a supply of liquor and had buried it in a snow bank at the side of the driveway. For some reason, her father, decided to clear the snow. Poor Nicola always got caught, while her sisters, she tells us, were smart enough to get away with murder. On that particular New Year's Eve, due to over-consumption of the discovered stash, she was feeling out of sorts and missed the whole celebration.

As well as the hordes of kids who descended upon us, we had been approached to house international students from

Asia. We had as many as three at one time, and they were all great fun, although most of them were very studious and motivated. One of them, Agnes, studied for hours in the garden with an ice pack on her head, while Nicola and her friends were lounging around the pool. That's probably why Agnes got 99% in Calculus and why Nicola and her friends did not.

Our delightful Asian students—Agnes and Emmi.

We won't forget Emmi, who arrived from Japan wearing white ankle socks and looking as if butter wouldn't melt in her mouth. She quickly got in with the wrong crowd, and only four months after she arrived, John met her creeping into the house in the early hours of the morning dressed like a hooker. We learned that as soon as she knew we were asleep, she had been climbing out of the window and leading quite the nightlife. We called it, "The North Americanisation of Emmi," and had to call her mother to take her home.

Of course, the students were typical teenagers all of whom treated us like parents and pulled the wool over our eyes at every turn. Agnes's brother, Michael and another boy, Anders, came the following year after Nicola had left for France to become a nanny, and things quietened down considerably. As soon as he turned 17, Michael's parents sent him $50,000, insisting he use it to buy a B.M.W. He really wanted a sports car, but he explained to us that the only things his parents cared about were status and money. He lost his license within months, but then parked the car several blocks away and continued to drive to school, he believed without our knowledge. He was attending Collingwood and was stunned one morning when I drew up right behind him. When Agnes called the following year to tell us that he had been killed while street racing in Boston, we were devastated to have lost a boy who had been like a son to us.

Several of the students moved with us to the new house in West Vancouver, which we eventually built after we had sold the second lot in Lions Bay. One of those for whom we had a special affection was a Japanese boy, Nobuki, because, along with other attributes, he loved our old cat, Sam, when Sam was really a cat that only an owner could love. She was not an appealing looking animal by anyone's standards. She had lost an eye when only a kitten by means that never became clear. We had to assume that she had been attacked by a raccoon before she had become wily enough to confront her wild animal foes.

Nobuki liked to study with Sam's help.

As she aged, she developed arthritis and became deformed, but Nobuki and Sam enjoyed a very special relationship and spent many hours sleeping on the couch together, while our own children began to make excuses not to look after her when we traveled. We hope they won't feel the same way about us, when we become blind, arthritic and incontinent.

Sam lived to be almost 23-years-old, despite having spent most of her life in the wilds amongst cougars, coyotes and raccoons. She lived with us longer than our children and was there to celebrate our 25th wedding anniversary. John began to worry about what was going to become of her when we were gone, especially when Margaret sent news of a 39-year-old cat in Gloucester that was still going strong.

When it became obvious that she wasn't likely to live much longer, and we were leaving for a holiday in Britain, John dug a large hole in the garden and instructed the girls to bury her if she died while we were away. They were amazed by the size of the hole, and one of them asked, "Dad, why on earth did you dig it so big?"

"Well, I thought it was a good idea just in case Mum went first," he replied.

Another lovely Japanese student, Takako, joined us in the new house and really became a part of the family. On John's fiftieth birthday, keen to be an integral part of the celebration, she baked a cake, covered it with whipping cream and kept it in her closet for three days before presenting it to him. He didn't have the heart to disappoint her so ate it while she sat beside him and watched him take every last bite.

When the time came for her to return to Japan, she cried uncontrollably because she didn't want to leave us. It was gratifying to know that we had provided a loving home for her and all the other students, and it was certainly a worthwhile experience for us. My only regret is that over the years we have lost touch with many of them. My searches on Facebook have been fruitless—looking for Japanese and Chinese names is akin to looking for Joneses in Wales.

We knew that we had to return to Lions Bay the day we attended the funeral of one of my ambulance friends, Ellen. As

A tearful goodbye to Takako at the airport.

I was consoling her husband, he said to me, "I could never get through this without the support of my wonderful Lions Bay family." I realised, at that moment, that if we died where we were living the people around us would never know. We had not met any of them; we had no neighbourhood family. We had lived in West Vancouver for more years than we had intended, even moving into an apartment when the rental house sold. John, who was still waffling about where to live, used to look down to check if there were free seats at "Bean Around the World", before strolling over for our morning coffee. We eventually came to our senses, however, and returned home. We now refer to that period as, "our mid-life crisis."

My Welsh friend Di, who I had met though Barb and Dave and would later become my colleague and teaching partner, was by then, living in Lions Bay. We had tried for a long time to persuade her and her husband to move to the village, and she never misses an opportunity to remind me that when they finally acquiesced and bought the house next door to some other good friends, we moved into town. She got over it, though, and welcomed us back to the village by including us in a dinner group that she had formed through the discovery that her husband, Mike, and Tim, the Lions Bay electrician, had dated the same girl in Clacton-on-Sea. Old girlfriends can lead to surprising connections.

Some of those connections, unfortunately, weren't as sound as they might have been and Di, in the future, would find herself a new, more exciting partner.

Di hoped that this man—Daniel Craig—would be easier to handle.

Many of the old neighbours are still living here—including Berenice, who will be 100-years-old this year—and remember the good and bad old days. New ones have moved in over the years and quickly been welcomed into our family.

Flo, sadly, although she resisted, was forced to move out by a husband who was not prepared, as he aged, to spend any more of his time maintaining such a large house. While everyone could understand where he was coming from, none of us could imagine Flo moving into a condominium in Squamish. She had spent some years selling Real Estate, and when the house didn't sell for quite a while, we believed that she was intentionally scuppering any potential sale of her own home. If she was, we didn't blame her one bit. We know how devastated she was when that unique home in which she had lived for over 40 years eventually sold, and she had no option but to move. My hope is that Home Depot in Squamish will continue to stock a plentiful supply of rope.

I met her on the beach on Canada Day and both she and her daughter, Tanya, were in tears. I asked her recently if she still hankered after Lions Bay. Her quick answer was that in the four years she has lived in Squamish she has not made one friend. She has lots of acquaintances who she has met through her sister who lives there but not one in her neighbourhood. That answered my question and confirmed my belief that communities such as ours are hard to come by. I know that she would come back here tomorrow if that husband of hers would agree to it. How can he have so easily put all those good times behind him? His favourite expression following every wild event was, "I haven't had so much fun since the pigs ate my brother." I bet he is not having nearly as much fun these days.

Lions Bay is now not only safer but much more respectable and sophisticated than it was in pioneer times. We had always organised special events for the community—New Year's Day polar bear swims, Easter egg hunts, Canada Day celebrations, Remembrance Day services and Santa's breakfasts, but now we have a very committed group of people who run a very professional Arts Council which arranges so many annual events—Art in the Garden, Banner Painting competitions for adults and children and a Christmas Fair where residents can showcase their talents in art, music, literature and their home industries. As I write, we are celebrating the 50th anniversary of the incorporation of Lions Bay as a village, and Ute, the head of the Arts Council, and her crew are excelling at organising innovative events to mark the occasion.

It is said that Lions Bay ranks in the top five communities across Canada with the highest number of artistic people per capita, but it has still managed to maintain that same small neighbourhood feel. Where else in the world would you find a

Mayor who sends out a weekly bulletin to introduce us to and welcome all new-comers to our little paradise?

There is a wonderful story about a gentleman who arrived in Canada and was attempting to phone Heaven. He first tried from Toronto but was horrified by the cost. In Winnipeg, he was quoted the same high price, and so it was in every city from which he tried to phone until he arrived in Lions Bay. He thought that before he gave up, he would try one last time. When he asked the operator how much it would cost to phone Heaven she replied, "That will be only 25 cents, Sir."

"But I don't understand, how can it be so cheap when it is so expensive to call from other places in Canada?"

"That's because from Lions Bay it is just a local call," was the response.

CHAPTER NINETEEN

Fill your life with experiences and not things. Have stories to tell, not stuff to show!

— Anonymous

DESPITE OUR LACK OF money in the early days, we always believed in that philosophy, and when I look back through photograph albums full of smiling faces and overflowing with memories, I know that no amount of stuff could ever compare with the pleasure of reliving those unforgettable moments with family and friends.

Following that trip to Britain—I know it is probably not wise to bring it up again—that one when my home was sold behind my back—we did not return for nine years. Lack of money was probably the real reason, but perhaps there was also a little nervousness on my part about leaving John alone for any length of time in case I once again became homeless.

While I really missed England, in the intervening years we had memorable holidays with the Moores family at Canon Beach and on Hornby Island, and we took up camping. We have such happy memories of driving along in our station wagon, singing along with Ralph McTell, Roger Whittaker and John Denver with the music belting out from those old Super Eight tapes.

One of our "camping" trips about which the children may prefer not to be reminded was one where we drove down the coast road to San Francisco. One could purchase what were called Entertainment books for $30.00 in those days which gave families access to nice hotels for half price. Always looking for a bargain, we splashed out, so on that particular trip we could alternate between a tent and more comfortable accommodation. Prior to that, the children had always told us that we had an uncanny knack for booking into places which they referred to as "Seedy Sid's." This time, we planned to go in style. Without telling John, I had taken along the electric kettle and an electric fry-pan so that we could economise on some meals. Our first hotel stop was at the Hilton in Newport, Oregon.

This was not the Hilton, but at least the Denby china came along.

One morning, John had left the hotel for some reason and on returning along the hall was puzzled by a strong smell of bacon radiating throughout a hotel which, as far as he knew, wasn't offering a cooked breakfast on the eighth floor. He was a little horrified when he saw what I had been up to but didn't turn down a hearty breakfast of bacon, eggs, tomatoes, mushrooms and fried bread, although he sat nervously on the edge of his chair expecting that at any minute the management would arrive to throw us out. That morning, we were on the road much earlier than even John had planned.

By the time we arrived at our hotel in San Francisco after camping on and off for two weeks, we resembled a gang of hobos, and the station-wagon was in disarray. The children had just reached that age when they are easily embarrassed by their parents, so when we drew up to the front door of a posh hotel to be greeted by a uniformed valet, they all dived under the seats, and Nicola naively believed it might detract from the scene if she put on her best shoes. There was no escape; we had no option but to scuttle through the elaborate foyer carrying bundles of dirty clothing, along with a collection of half-washed pans, boxes of food and the electrical appliances.

In those years, we also enjoyed annual ski trips with the neighbours to Crystal Mountain in Washington, and our children will always treasure fond memories of the Silver Skis Chalet with its central heated pool, and all those pot-luck dinners. As with the Christmas dinners at Max and Val's, the numbers eventually became so unwieldy that it was impossible for us all to get together for meals, but a few families continued the tradition, taking along their grandchildren, until it became easier and cheaper to ski in Canada.

It was undoubtedly the Gienger family who encouraged us to join the skiing fraternity by taking a week-long Headway Course at Grouse Mountain which had to be one of the most painful and humiliating experiences of our lives. It began well enough with the purchase of fashionable one-piece ski suits. It only took John four years to find out why his had been made in such a way that it was difficult for him to use the bathroom. I suppose I wasn't really paying attention, probably because I was having to get myself and three children kitted out and on the slopes by 8.30 a.m. while he was involved in the arduous task of getting just himself ready. I should have twigged when he said, "I wonder why they make these ski suits in such a stupid way that you have to take them off to go for a pee?" The penny didn't drop until the day Flo said to him, "John, I've been wondering why you always wear your ski suit back to front?"

John's idea of a ski trip, with the Fleming girls, Dorothy, Mamie and Flo.

Rose's idea of a ski trip—matching hand-knitted toques for all.

But we did hit the slopes by 8:30 a.m. every day—Crystal Mountain, Washington, USA

Within the first five minutes of the first ski lesson on Grouse, both of us were assigned to the lowest class along with a Chinese gentleman and a recent Polish immigrant. We had been asked to ski down the gentlest of slopes and turn right at the bottom. John went first, and despite the fact that he was leaning his body as far to the right as he possibly could, he turned left and disappeared out of sight down a bank, followed in hot pursuit by the Chinese gentleman. As they struggled to extricate themselves from each other's tangled bodies and a jumble of skis, the ski instructor shook his head knowingly. "It's a strange thing," he said, "but I always have trouble trying to teach English and Chinese people to ski." I was willing to accept then and there, that we were of the wrong nationality and much too old to take up such a dangerous sport.

Because we had booked lessons for the week, however, we had no option but to persevere, despite the icy conditions that we believed were normal, excruciatingly painful rental boots, bruised bodies and in my case, a brand-new ski-suit ripped to shreds. By the end of the week, we were ready to progress to the Cut, which is an easy beginners' slope, but to us resembled the side of the Matterhorn. "Keep straight and to the middle," warned the instructor which all of us managed to execute perfectly except for the poor Chinese gentleman who skied straight into the snowmaker and hit his nose. While he bled profusely, and the hill began to look like a battle scene, I was forced to disappear into the bushes to conceal my mirth.

The sight of someone hurt or bleeding has always, for some bizarre reason, caused me to burst into uncontrollable fits of laughter. This seemed abnormal, especially for an ambulance attendant, but I have discovered it is fairly common for people to cry or laugh in a situation that most people wouldn't find amusing. Medical experts even have a name for it—they would, wouldn't they? It's called Pseudobulbar Affect or PBA. Since acronyms became popular in the 1960s, everything unpronounceable seems to have one, so now, when anyone asks why I am laughing hysterically while they are bleeding to death I can say, "I'm sorry, I suffer from PBA."

Immediately following that course, the Giengers took us on a ski trip to three B.C. ski resorts after which, having reached a rather basic level of proficiency, we had the audacity to believe that we were ready to teach the children. It surprises me that no one got injured or killed during that first season while we fell from chairs, wiped out whole lines of people waiting to load, crashed into trees and other skiers and generally caused mayhem.

John made one of the most spectacular exoduses from the chair, that should have been entered in the Guinness Book of Records. He hadn't been told that he could ski on the green matting when leaving the chair. He waited until he was beyond it and over the snow. By that time, he was 15 to 20 feet in the air, and he thought there was no option but to jump for it. He reached the snow but lay there in agony unable to get up while the next six or seven people skied gracefully down on the matting and wiped out on top of him. The chair had to be halted for an embarrassingly long time until the mess of bodies was cleared out of the way. It was a hard way to learn.

Despite those early experiences, we persevered, and we continue to enjoy the sport to this day. In our seventies, John and I even joined what was erroneously called a "Seniors' Ski

Team"—a one-day-a-week session for the elderly where we were placed in groups based on our level of expertise. Those lessons were so much fun, and really upped our game.

It is second nature for Canadians to deal with ice and snow, and I have never met one who doesn't know how to skate. Our ski instructor had left us in no doubt about our aptitude for winter sports, but that didn't deter us when Harold found a frozen lake way up in the mountains where he had been logging and suggested a skating party in the moonlight.

Some of the old Whistler ski bunnies!

We all piled into his crummy—a crew cab used to transport logging crews to the site—and he drove many miles up to a mountain lake, through trees hanging in tiers of frozen snow glittering in the moonlight. With a huge stretch of the imagination, it could have been a scene from Dr. Zhivago. I don't need to go into detail about John's and my skating experience because you will have automatically assumed that it was disastrous. The girls tried to drag us around in our rented skates, but our ankles seemed to have suddenly become weak.

Nevertheless, it was a magical evening roasting marshmallows over a huge bonfire, watching the Canadians gliding gracefully around the ice in the moonlight and listening to the coyotes howling across the lake. "Quintessentially Canadian," John's Dad would have said.

I had forgotten just how much time we spent on the slopes at Whistler.

CHAPTER TWENTY

Our business in life is not to get ahead of others but to get ahead of ourselves.

— E. Joseph Cossman

NOT BEING PEOPLE WITH airs and graces or too proud to engage in menial tasks, before I returned to teaching, we increased our income by taking on little jobs that just seemed to fall into our laps.

With so much time off, John was invited to moonlight on the B.C. Ferries which left us in no doubt about how the NDP government was wasting taxpayers' money. He was frequently called out on public holidays and paid double time. His favourite trip was the 32-minute run from Horseshoe Bay to Snug Cove on Bowen Island requiring little in the way of navigational skills. After three trips, the boat would be tied up for the crew to take a "needed" two-hour rest. If John did a late trip to the Sunshine Coast, he was paid to stay overnight in a hotel, but often, he would be given the money for the accommodation and then told to hitch a ride on the return ferry. I thought this was highly immoral, and I know John G doesn't want to hear stories like this because he still gets annoyed about the number of times he called John at the office in working hours, only to be told that he was probably outside washing his car. When he heard of John's plan to retire, John G scoffed, "Retire from what exactly? You've never really worked a day in your life!"

At some point, my husband was asked by his squash partner to be a stand-in for his friend's job as a quality control representative for Robins' do-nuts. That job gave us opportunities to stay in nice hotels around B.C. On one trip to Vancouver Island, we dragged along a couple of donut-loving friends who were able to share our room with two queen size beds, and enjoy donuts for breakfast, mid-morning snack, lunch and afternoon tea. We were all soon experiencing an extreme sugar high and discovered what living life in the fast lane really meant. Alas, at the end of John's second year of donut tasting, he just couldn't take it anymore and has never been able to enter a donut establishment since.

He and his office colleagues, all of whom only worked alternate weeks, then started a landscaping company which they called "All Seasons' Landscaping." That was a misnomer seeing that they only operated from May to September when the weather wasn't inclement. Despite the fact that none of them knew the difference between a weed and a flower—one of the men called every flower "a posie"—they conned quite a few people into allowing them to do expensive projects on their properties. They purchased an old dump truck and watched with self-satisfaction as the garbage tipped out with a mere pull of a lever while other poor sods were shovelling theirs out by hand. I think John really enjoyed that feeling of being king of the dump.

Wayne, the supplier of John's second-hand jeans, was a star at finding well-used but useful articles amongst the trash. Along with a good pair of working boots and a few other questionable treasures, John became the proud owner of a Deutsche Grammophon collection of "only slightly damaged" Beethoven Symphonies. He still becomes a little tense, when anticipating the click as the needle hits the scratch on the second movement of Beethoven's Pastoral.

When Nicola entered Grade One, I returned to teaching, but it was really too soon, being the all-consuming profession that it is. Things were not so demanding during John's time off from the office, but when he was called home to England for weeks to be with his dying father, it became onerous. The last straw was when the car broke down in the middle of the highway on our way to visit Flo's parents in Chilliwack. I handed in my resignation and became a teachers' aide at the local school.

Following a teachers' strike around 1980, all teachers' aides were made redundant which was when the other aide, Judy, suggested we start a cleaning company. I almost got fired by one of our clients because I kept hiding their ugly door-mat which would never lie flat so offended my sensibilities, and they had the audacity to accuse me of taking liberties above my station.

We were also asked if we would like to take over the morning paper route, and when we learned that the stipend for delivering just 36 papers in an hour was half of what I would be offered for a full-time job at Collingwood School in 1985, we jumped at the opportunity. The disasters that resulted from that experience could fill a book by themselves. As most of the papers got thrown from the car window, they ended up in some interesting places—bushes, drains, flower-beds but rarely doorsteps, and one actually ended up on someone's roof. One morning when it was bitterly cold, Helen managed to throw one onto an interior doormat; hurled at the glass front door, it went straight through, leaving a round hole just the size of the rolled newspaper. The owners were astounded to find it waiting in the freezing front hall when they got up.

We still clearly remember the morning that Helen came running down the hall shouting, "Dad something terrible has happened to the car." Backing down a steep driveway, she had managed to get two of the wheels hanging precipitously over the edge. The tow-truck arrived and managed to retrieve the car from the bank where it had been in danger of tumbling onto an expensive one parked below. A neighbour, Jennifer, who kindly took over the paper route while we were in England on our next adventure was not so lucky. She almost destroyed her car when it went completely over the edge of a steep driveway wiping out far more than her income from the job.

Phone the tow-truck company! Another paper route cheque down the tube!

Following the near catastrophes, John came up with a really addle-brained idea; he thought it would be safer if we bought a small motor-bike so that we could all "zip up and down the roads safely and turn more easily at the top of driveways." He estimated that we would also be able to do the route in half the time.

It didn't take long to reveal that I was just not a natural on a motorbike; I could never get used to the idea of pulling the throttle towards me to accelerate and turning it away from me to brake. One morning, as I was heading towards a huge tree, in my effort to brake, I accelerated further and further up the trunk until I had to let go when my arms would stretch no higher. I fell on my back with the motorbike engine still running on top of me.

John thought he had mastered the machine in record time, until he encountered black ice, one morning. The bike shot out from under him, and his newspapers flew out of the Dairyland box and scattered all over the road and into the ditch. The motorbike was still purring along nicely as he slid around on the ice, searching for the papers in the dark.

Hurtling along with a Dairyland milk crate strapped behind.

After that disaster, he went out in deep snow in a little Nissan Micra that we owned and found that it was brilliant going backwards on the hills, so in that way, he was able to cover most of the village in record time.

Because part of the route was along the main highway, we realised that we needed to have a license and would have to take a test. John believed he was more than ready, but I was in no doubt that I was not. Nevertheless, we booked an appointment together.

We were instructed to wear heavy leather gloves and boots for the test, items that we didn't own, so we borrowed gauntlet style gloves and a pair of cowboy boots from our neighbour, Harold, that were many sizes too large. They were so cumbersome that I could not feel the controls, and I wiped out several of the orange cones that I was asked to steer around. John who was watching, assumed that I had failed the test and appeared even to be gloating a little until his turn came.

He decided to show off and drive around the cones at high speed, whereupon he sent them flying in all directions before coming to a dramatic stop with the last cone wedged firmly under the bike. I was the one gloating then, as I watched John and the examiner trying to extricate the cone which I am sure was used as a visual aid for future students taking a test.

Crestfallen and somewhat embarrassed, we loaded the bike back into our jeep and drove slowly home wondering what our next move should be. The motorbike sold the following week without Helen ever being given an opportunity to take a test, and we all agreed that it was high time to hand over the paper route to some other unfortunate soul. Thank you, Nancy!

John had a knack for coming up with zany ideas, but I will admit that I probably won the contest for coming up with the zaniest, in the year 2000. There not being any accommodation in Lions Bay for visitors, we had occasionally opened our home as a B&B for couples who were visiting for weddings or other family events, and we had enjoyed the experience. I was, therefore, thinking ahead to getting involved in some enterprise along those lines that would be lucrative, but give us plenty of flexibility to travel following my retirement from Collingwood.

We started a company, called "Canhike" which offered a week's accommodation along with a week of hiking. The idea was to house couples for three days in Lions Bay and three days at our Whistler chalet. Each day, I would supply full breakfasts, a packed lunch, and dinner every evening. John would organise daily hikes. Because I was teaching full-time, we only planned to operate in July and August until I retired and in alternate weeks when John was not working. We were quite prepared to do all the work ourselves for the first season but then hoped to hire staff and sit back and enjoy the profits. We advertised in the London Times and Country Life, believing that those subscribers would be able to afford our exorbitant prices.

In the first season, three couples signed up. As it turned out, while I was killing myself in the kitchen, John was killing them on the hikes. The week's programme included five hikes —Goat Mountain, above Grouse, Mt. Gardener on Bowen

Island, Diamond Head, Joffre Lakes and Whistler Peak—a gruelling schedule even for Iron Man types.

When we sized up the first couple at the airport, we knew we were doomed; we guessed that their previous hiking experience had been no more than ambles from the car, across the parking lot into the grocery store. Nevertheless, on the first morning, John accompanied them up the gondola at Grouse Mountain and then led them to the top of Goat Mountain for what he termed, "a gentle hike," just less than 1,000 ft. On the way down, the woman was so tired she stumbled and did a face plant in the snow, and as John dug her out, he began to worry about potential court cases. The couple and John came home knackered, the guests, physically, and John, mentally.

While they were falling asleep at the dinner table, we suggested that they have an early night because the following morning they were being taken to Bowen Island to hike to the top of Mount Gardner at 2,470 ft. We told them they should take it easy on that hike because on day three it was going to be "a bit of a slog" up Diamond Head. They were already crying out in agony when being helped downstairs, so our hopes were not high that they would complete what was really an "Outward Bound" course. Moving on to Whistler on day four, they still had to complete a hike to Joffre Lakes and to the Peak at Whistler—a mere 6,903 ft—on day five.

The next guests were two lovely ladies from Australia who were much fitter, but still not up to such unreasonable expectations. They really did put their best foot forward, however, and only balked on day three.

The last couple who came from Scotland were the only ones to complete the course, but on the last hike in typical Scottish weather, with swirling mists and pouring rain, the man suddenly slumped over a huge boulder unable to walk another step. When his wife divulged that her husband had suffered a heart attack the previous year, I looked at John who was so pale I was sure that he was about to have one. Somehow, we managed to coach that poor man down the mountain. Surprisingly, his wife still keeps in touch, sending us a Christmas card every year, and on two occasions she has met up with us in Scotland. She is still so complimentary about "their unforgettable experience." Some people really are gluttons for punishment, particularly the Scots, it would appear.

That couple left at the end of August, barely able to walk, just one day before I had to return to Collingwood to prepare for the new term. I thought that "Canhike" should be changed to "Can't Hike," or we should quit while we were ahead. We quit, and I admitted that it had been a failed experiment. All that remains of that lark are two coffee mugs with the Canhike logo that Helen designed for us.

All that remains of our ill-fated business venture.

You may not be surprised to learn that John had kept a careful account of all our expenditures and our profit. The "Canhike/Can't hike" income came to $7,826 and the expenses were $6,511, giving us a net gain of $1,315. Perhaps we should have persevered with that idea because most would-be entrepreneurs don't expect to make any profit during the first few years.

Despite having proved without a doubt that we were not suited for entrepreneurial endeavours, some years later we found ourselves unable to resist dabbling around the fringes once again.

Lions Bay friends who can give the Jollymores a run for their money when it comes to creativity, invited us to a Hippie Be-In requesting that we bring "some cool hippie product to share with like-minded groovy friends."

A party invitation to embrace our past inner hippie selves

John was dying to showcase his purple, checked bellbottoms, realising that this was a golden opportunity, but they couldn't be found. "I can't believe someone would have the audacity to throw out my favourite pants," he grumbled, but I didn't think it was such a big deal because he had lots of other choices that had been hanging in his closet since the sixties.

Our hosts lured us with the words, "whatever your imagination can conjure up." Well, we were already aware that our imaginations can run riot, and since John had already been going through his "save the world from extinction faze" for some time, we decided to go the whole hog and make our own biodegradable, all-natural laundry detergent and hand around samples in matching, recycled instant coffee jars. We called it "DUD'S SUDS," and I designed a fancy label for each jar which boasted of its superior, world-saving properties.

Proud not to be "in vogue"—hippie duds straight from the closet.

Easy to tell that most of this mob had lived through the Hippie era.

Save the world with DUD's SUDS!

Initially, I believe everyone was impressed, and once we had begun to use it ourselves, we thought that we had hit on something earth-shattering. Unfortunately, within the first month, the "fair trade vegan soap with organic oils" had completely bunged up the washing machine and very soon it, along with "DUD'S SUDS," went down the drain.

Well, not quite all of our ventures ran smoothly, but as a team, we had always been prepared to make sacrifices, to work hard and accomplish whatever was necessary to take charge of our financial future. This last venture, surprisingly, brought in no income at all, but the extra money that we earned from all our earlier endeavours had allowed us to pay off the mortgage in eight years and reap the fruits of our labour from then on.

CHAPTER TWENTY-ONE

Travel is the best school; it has the best teacher because everything seen is a teacher; and this colourful school's diploma is wisdom.

— Mehmet Murat ildan

Our "not a pot to piss in" days were behind us.

OUR NEXT VACATION TO Europe in 1981 was quite the trip. Over a seven-week period, apart from visiting England and

Wales, we took the children on an educational tour of five European countries ending in Athens from where we flew back to London. Our "not a pot to piss in" days were far behind us. It was the first trip to England for Nicola, and it cost much more than our Richmond home.

Welcome home poster made by Tanya and the Shand girls.

We received such a wonderful welcome from the neighbours on our return which mitigated some of my sadness on leaving my homeland behind once more.

In 1984, we drove across France and Spain staying in wonderful old monasteries and castles that had been converted into hotels—no more "Seedy Sids" for us! That was the one and only time we stayed at an apartment that we had bought on impulse in Nerja, near Malaga, when we had been on holiday in England and had become tired of the incessant rain. At that time, since we had met in Spain and had a special affinity for everything Spanish, we had this ridiculous notion that we would retire there. A few years later, we realised that impulse buying is a foolish idea and sold the apartment to buy our Whistler ski chalet. It is a little closer to home so can be enjoyed by the whole family on a regular basis.

Back to killer drinks at the local bar.

Stacey and Dawn's Welcome Home cake

Rose Dudley

Jon of Sliding Fireplace is so happy we've returned.

The road less travelled—John's idea of heaven—at 12,000 ft in the Sierra Nevada, Spain.

We have such happy memories of our family holidays, but inevitably, the time came when our girls lost interest in travelling with their parents. I still remember how shocked I was while organising our next adventure, when Alison told me that she was making her own arrangements with friends. Of course, they were more than happy to return to the fold when they all had families of their own. We have had several holidays, all fifteen of us together, and it is my hope that we will have many more before John and I kick the bucket.

Certainly, friends play a huge role in everyone's life, but especially for those like us who have moved to a new country and no longer have families to lean on. We have been fortunate to have been surrounded by good friends with whom we can enjoy holidays.

We, along with the Enns's felt like an extension of the Gienger family when we were invited to take the train to Flo's brother's wedding, along with about 20 of their relatives, in Drayton Valley, Alberta. We have always enjoyed train travel,

Arriving in Drayton Valley, Alberta.

but had never been on a train in Canada. We were excited about going through the Rockies but reached them in darkness. It was a beautiful, clear night, and I remember seeing their ghostly, snow-capped outlines in the moonlight as we peered out of our bunks, and hearing the click on the rails as we slowly chugged through the mountain passes.

When we arrived at our destination, we were all quite taken aback as we were dropped off in the snow beside the tracks in the middle of nowhere, and the train continued its journey across that vast white landscape, sounding its haunting whistle. I thought I had just arrived from the boonies, but now I really understood the meaning of the word. I thought back to the "Howdy Pardner" sign that had alarmed me at the Calgary airport on my arrival in Canada in 1967. Now, I really felt as if we were in cowboy country. The snow-covered prairies stretched out for miles in every direction.

A bus arrived to take us into the little town of Drayton Valley where the bride, Gwen, lived and worked as a pharmacist. The only thing I can remember about the town was the huge funeral parlour close to our motel, but there must

When in Drayton Valley

have been other stores because both Harold and David bought cowboy hats to blend in with the locals.

Terry, Flo's brother, was obviously marrying into a family much like his own—one where everyone is welcome to "pull up a stump," and numbers are of no consequence—the more the merrier. Gwen's family had not only invited us to the wedding but included us in all the pre and post wedding events. The girls remember that as one of their favourite trips.

Another journey that we took by train was to Quesnel, 650 km north of us, for a dog-sledding holiday at Kruger Lake. Until 2002, a passenger train ran through Lions Bay— a former flag stop—all the way to Prince George. It was a breathtaking journey through varied and stunning countryside, and it is such a shame that the service has been discontinued. We were on the train the whole day and were continually supplied with food and beverages. The driver slowed or stopped the train to point out mountain goats perched on the hills above us, and anything else of interest.

From Quesnel, we were bussed to Wells which was once a thriving mining town, and the following morning we travelled by snowmobile to the outfitter's cabin on Kruger Lake.

The accommodation was very basic. All six of us—the Goulds, Max and his daughter Katie, and John and I—slept in one big cabin, and the outhouse was at some distance away through deep snow. It wasn't a popular walk during the night, which became obvious as the snow changed colour around the accommodation throughout the week.

Our hosts were delightful and provided us with hearty meals of moose steaks—that must now be one of John's more unpleasant memories. In the corner of the living room was a huge stuffed grizzly bear that the host's Dad had shot as it attacked him near the lake.

The dogs that would pull our sleds were kept in separate kennels because they fought with each other and were impossible to separate. Each night, they stood on the roofs of their kennels and howled at the moon.

Each couple was given a team of six Alaskan Malamutes to pull the sleds through the countryside. One would sit in the sled while the other acted as musher. Since I had only, the day before we left, had my cast removed after breaking my leg in a ski accident, I had to sit while John mushed, On the third day, I was dying to try mushing so with John sitting in the sled I tried to push off, but my leg was so weak that it gave out on me. I lay prostrate in the snow watching the dogs tear off with no driver and John trying to climb over the back to get into a position where he could grab the reins and operate the brake. It was like a scene from the Keystone Cops. His team ran so fast that they caught up with another team and all hell broke loose as they tried to control twelve snarling dogs. It was certainly a trip to remember!

Practising for the Iditarod

CHAPTER TWENTY-TWO

Returning home is the most difficult part of long-distance hiking. You have grown outside the puzzle and your piece no longer fits.

— Cindy Ross

WHEN I READ THAT quote, it hit a chord with me. At the culmination of our long-distance hikes, we have all experienced such a sense of loss—almost a feeling of withdrawal—and have had difficulty fitting back into our normal routine. There is nothing more liberating than carrying just a few essentials on one's back, having rid oneself of the unnecessary trappings of life. The mystery is why, having had such an experience, we all seem so determined to force that puzzle piece back into place.

We have had many walking adventures in Britain and Europe, as well as frequent holidays with our families there. The long-distance hikes in England and Wales are those that have kept me sane and helped me to accept my life in Canada, but I had to wait for 34 years, until I retired in 2001, to return in the spring, to recapture the beauty and fragrance of bluebell woods and flower-lined country lanes.

Our first long-distance hike around 30 years ago, was on the Coast to Coast Path—from St. Bees Head to Robin Hood's Bay—a distance of 293 km which we completed in 11 days.

Rose Dudley

And it only took us 20 years to complete!

Starting out on the Cotswold Way.

That was much too fast, because the beauty of the English countryside is to be savoured, but two of our hiking companions needed to catch a plane.

The Tilley hat brigade on stage two of the South West Coastal Path. John's must have blown off along the way.

The British brain drain—Canada must have been desperate!

Since then, we have tackled most of the long-distance paths, each one seemingly more beautiful than the previous one. It never ceases to amaze us how few long-distance walkers we encounter, and how easy it is to get away from crowds in a country that is so overpopulated.

Meeting up with the Hills on the Sussex hills—South Downs Way.

Because we enjoy long-distance walks and have a love of Spain, we knew that one day we would tackle the 804-km El Camino de Santiago, but my teaching schedule meant that we could only do it in Spain's hottest summer months. After my retirement, however, we were free to go in spring when the temperature was more favourable, and en route, as I said previously, delight in those bluebell woods in Wales that I had been missing for 34 years. Another thrill, which we had not expected, was to hear the cuckoo's call every day as we trudged along the trail.

El Camino de Santiago—the Way of St. James—is a network of Christian routes all leading to the cathedral in Santiago where the body of St. James is purported to be buried. The story goes that St. James, one of Jesus's disciples, was transported to the north coast of Spain in a stone boat, and his bones were eventually brought to the cathedral. Our trek was

Catching up with more of the Wray clan on the West Highland Way.

Andrea and Graham had shrunk by the last stage of the South West Coast Path.

neither intended as a Christian pilgrimage, nor as a means to find ourselves as it is for many. Our affinity with Spain began with our meeting there, but many of the people we befriended were dealing with some inner conflict and were more than ready to share their stories. One of the more tormented souls was Dominique, a flautist, who played in churches along the way, turning the walk into a near spiritual experience for us. Apart from Dominique, we met up with others with whom we have been in touch ever since. Mona and Eoin provided plenty of typically Irish humour every day. By coincidence, they came from the same town in Donegal as my Irish family. When I told them that we had been to the cemetery in their town to visit the graves of my grandparents and other relatives, Oein said, "I probably put some of those relatives in that graveyard." We assumed that he must be the town gravedigger, but as we got to know him, we learned that he was the local GP who had treated my cousin, who I had never met, but who, I learned from Eoin, was suffering from Multiple Sclerosis. One often hears stories of "unusual coincidences and happenings" that people experience while walking along the Camino, and being Welsh, I

Iron sculpture by Mencia Rodriguez.

do tend to be superstitious, but prior to that incident we had both been somewhat sceptical.

There are many Pilgrim-themed sculptures all along El Camino but a stunning one which is impossible to miss is a work by Mencia Rodriguez fashioned in iron, on Alto del Perdon. High on a windy hill, it depicts twelve Pilgrims, through the ages, with the last modern-day one carrying a backpack. The wording on the accompanying plaque is very appropriate: "Donde se cruza el camino del viento con el de las estrellas"—Where the path of the wind crosses that of the stars.

Although the official walk ends in Santiago, many 'pilgrims" continue on to Cabo Finisterra which the Celts call "The End of the Earth." Being a Celt, that stretch was important. There is a spot there where it is the custom to burn one's running shoes or boots, but we are far too cheap to have done something so wasteful. Mine would be good for at least another 800 km.

A few years later, we tackled the Tour de Mont Blanc with our Irish friends. Mona told us she had come armed with something called "Rescue Remedy." We thought she was joking, but she wasn't, and it came in very handy on the ladders. Some

"The Group of Seven"—friends we made on El Camino.

She couldn't have done it without "Rescue Remedy."

"Rescue Remedy" or not—Mitchi, Gerry and I bailed out.

years later, I discovered it was available in Canada, and my writing teacher kept a bottle of it on the desk for people who were nervous about sharing their written work.

How I love reliving my childhood on those trips to Britain and Europe and feeling rejuvenated from being in open countryside beneath expansive blue skies. Since John started regular Monday hikes, it is always so difficult for me to return and muster up any enthusiasm for trekking off into a dark rainforest. To me it is akin to being hurled back into a dank, dark prison cell after being allowed out for a fleeting taste of sunshine. His response is to laugh and say, "Get over it!" He will never truly understand why I don't completely share his love of the wilderness that supposedly brought him here. That feeling of being swallowed whole is offset only through our stunning view of the ocean and faraway islands, and the light and beauty of the endless sky which uplifts the spirit within me.

CHAPTER TWENTY-THREE

Every time I see an adult on a bicycle I no longer despair for the future of the human race.

— H.G. Wells

WELL, IF H.G. WELLS were around in North America today, he would be wallowing in the depths of despair. It is only in recent years that Vancouver has embraced cycling to any extent, and with much opposition from those who are reluctant to forsake their car dependence. When the highway to Whistler was being upgraded for the 2010 Olympics, what an ideal opportunity it would have been to build a long-distance, dedicated bike path, but the government missed a golden opportunity. It disheartens me to see how reluctant Canadian cities have been to recognise that cycling is not only healthier for humans and the environment, but those long-distance paths provide a boost for the economy. Gregor Robertson, a former Mayor, in his effort to make Vancouver a "Green" city, did much to improve cycling infrastructure, but not without constant verbal abuse from the motoring fraternity who need to embrace the truth that "Four wheels move the body. Two wheels move the soul."

Cycling gives one that same feeling of freedom as long-distance walking, but I would never consider taking my life in my hands on Canada's roads. When we wish to take a cycling holiday, we choose to go to Holland, Germany or Austria. Cycling in Europe is such a pleasure on the dedicated bike paths that have been an integral part of the European culture for decades and frequently built in much more challenging terrain.

Cycling beside the Danube looking for Kaffe and Kuchen.

And there it is!—always just around the next corner.

Did he really think they sold Schnitzel? "They've run out," he said.

Climb every mountain—shades of "The Sound of Music," in Austria.

In Holland, one can leave the airport in Amsterdam and find a dedicated bike path right outside the entrance doors

Bikes returned—off on the next adventure!

which leads to a network of lanes all across the country and into Belgium.

The paths along the rivers in Germany are so family friendly, and cycling along by the Danube is a breeze, but on a trip to Austria in 2016, we found the cycling more of a challenge. Nevertheless, the experience of riding on safe, dedicated bike paths is a joy that one can only dream about in Vancouver.

When John and I left the other members of our group in Salzburg, the real meaning of the word "challenge" hit us as we cycled on to Prague and were forced to tackle a 23 km ascent out of the Danube valley from Linz, on the second day.

Moving out of our comfort zone, and encouraged by a couple of bred-in-the-bone cycling friends, Per and Eva, we took our bikes to Cuba. Alison was between jobs so able to join us, and her fluent Spanish was an asset.

Cuba is a wonderful country for tourists who choose to cycle, because of the U.S oil embargo which keeps motorised traffic off the roads, but not for those who have suffered for years under U.S. restraints.

It is easy for visitors to get an entirely wrong impression of a country—it has an excellent health care system, high levels of education in all fields, and is the only country that meets sustainable development targets, but, at the same time, any dissenters are repressed and punished, and free speech is not tolerated. The wages are so low that many professional people are reduced to menial labour. We came across many of them—doctors, lawyers and teachers etc.—running state-controlled Casas Particulares—B&Bs.

Argentinian born Che Guevara, Fidel Castro's second in command when they overthrew the Batista dictatorship in January 1959, is still a hero in Cuba, and everywhere posters of him are on display including a huge one in the Plaza de la Revolution in Havana. Being of leftist leanings ourselves, we embraced the history of the small group of 82 men who landed in Cuba on the leaky old cabin cruiser, the Granma, in November 1956. Only 22 of them survived, but in three years, they had beaten the U.S. backed dictatorship.

They will never forget Che in Cuba.

The verdict is still out on whether Che Guevara is, in fact, a hero. He is thought of as a terrorist by many, but that didn't stop Alison from stashing quite a bit of Che memorabilia into her pannier as gifts for her like-minded friends.

We cycled down the Bay of Pigs and took great delight in visiting the museum which commemorates the defeat of the U.S. in that battle by that name, in three short days.

By coincidence, John was a cadet on an old British freighter called the Pampas that docked in Havana in February 1962, the day that the U.S. announced they would not be importing any more Cuban goods. As he walked around the city, the shops were almost bare, but had posters of a defiant Fidel and Nikita Kruschev displayed in their windows, and many young men and women with sub-machine guns patrolling the streets.

We have also enjoyed so many wonderful adventures with the Norwesters' Seniors' Cycle Group. I joined them when I retired in 2001, and John became a member on his retirement a few years later.

He will not forget the first trip he ever did with the group. Most of the cyclists stayed at a campsite, but we opted for the comfort of a hotel. When we turned up the next morning

A few of the original members of the cycling club.

Cycling can be risky—two broken wrists for Sue in Riccione, Italy.

A group of Norwesters cycling El Camino.

prepared for the first ride, John surveyed all the old men and women hobbling around the campsite in head-to-toe spandex

An unforgettable trip to New Zealand with Stan, our fearless leader. The last great adventure, prior to the lock-down.

and thought, "Whatever is a young, fit guy like me doing here with these people?"

When they mounted their expensive, carbon-fibre bikes and took off at speeds reaching 40 km an hour, he realised that he would need to do some intensive training in the future, to keep up with those people in their 70s and 80s. Reaching our destination at a town 45 km away, most of the riders leaped from their saddles and dived into the lake for a swim before lunch. John snuck into the Harrison Hot Springs Hotel and fell fast asleep on a couch in the lobby. Someone had to shake him awake to give him the good news that it was only a 45-km- ride back to our hotel.

Two of the most inspiring members of the cycling group are Joyce and Bud, seen in the picture below. Joyce at 85, and I, at 80, along with my daughter, Alison, aged 50, had planned to tackle the Whistler Gran Fondo together in 2021, to celebrate all those milestones, but, due to the pandemic, we may have to wait until the following year. Alison and I completed that 132 km ride in 2016.

Rose Dudley

Back from a 75 km ride, and these two super-seniors, now 84 and 90, look as fresh as daisies.

CHAPTER TWENTY-FOUR

The best way to find yourself is to lose yourself in the service of others.

— Mahatma Ghandi

SEVERAL OF OUR HOLIDAYS have incorporated volunteer opportunities in South and Central America with two wonderful organisations. Project Hands was started by an anaesthetist and his wife and daughter here in Lions Bay to provide needed surgeries for the Indigenous people of Guatemala, and in more recent years to those in Bolivia. We also worked briefly with an organisation called Wells of Hope which had been started by a Dutch-born Canadian, Ted Vanderzalm, who has spent years providing clean water for the Indigenous people in Guatemala and building schools there, as well as supporting orphanages.

As part of a group from Canada, the women created a garden for one orphanage while John and some others retiled a floor that had been raised by overflowing sewage through which children as young as two-years-old were toddling, dragging security blankets through the detritus.

We then dug a septic field for a school where over 300 students had been limited to one filthy out-house, and we assisted in the building of a school where children had been, up to then, educated out of doors often in the blistering heat. We felt such pride on seeing those Canadian flags on at least seven schools as we drove to our work sites. Observing the gratitude in waves and shouts of "Hola Ted, Como estas tu?" as we drove through the villages, and sitting down to a hearty chicken meal provided by those who couldn't afford to eat meat themselves but wanted to show us their appreciation was heart-warming. One day, Ted drove us to a cemetery where he pointed out hundreds of tiny graves. With a lump in his throat he mumbled, "All of those children died from water-borne diseases; every eight seconds one dies somewhere in the world." The silence was palpable as we drove back to his home.

Digging septic fields can be fun when one has a mission!

It is one thing to have the opportunity to participate in volunteer work, but those who initiate such ventures are the ones to be admired. Our friends in Lions Bay, who recognised the need for medical aid in Guatemala, carrying out necessary operations on those who had been unable to continue working to feed their families, and Ted who saw the need to provide clean water to reduce the number of children lying in that cemetery are the real heroes.

Senora Project Hands herself, with Debbie and Aurelio.

The whole P.H. team in Camanchaj, Guatemala

Guatemala is another beautiful country with an unfortunate history, beginning with the Spanish Conquest in 1524. It became an independent country in 1841. It is one of those countries where the United Fruit Company, supported by authoritarian rulers and the U.S.A., brought in brutal labour relations and massive concessions to the wealthy. The people are still struggling from the effects of a thirty-year civil war, ending only in 1997, and mass genocide of the Indigenous Mayan population by the military. Extreme poverty amongst the Indigenous groups is widespread, and drug-induced crime is rampant. We were all warned not to venture out after dark.

CHAPTER TWENTY-FIVE

Go canoeing with your wife," they said. "Nothing will go wrong", they said.

— Unknown

WHOEVER SAID THAT HAD obviously never been canoeing with his wife, and none of us heeded the advice before we took off to the Bowron Lakes situated 700 km north of Vancouver.

The Lakes are popular because one can canoe all seven with short portages in between and arrive back at the beginning. Sadly, they are so in demand these days that it is necessary to book months in advance to have the opportunity, but that wasn't the case when we arranged to go canoeing there along with three other couples with only one of the couples having had much previous experience.

It was the first time we had met Basil and Tish Davis, through John G and Chris, and we knew immediately that they were our kind of people—people who would be not averse to roughing it at times.

We had to break the journey at a motel en route, and that was where John G lost one of his front teeth—something he seems to have a habit of doing. He looked like Fagin from Oliver Twist, someone who you wouldn't want to be seen with, but what option did we have? We tried to pretend that he wasn't with us for the next week.

A group of mostly canoeing neophytes heading for disaster.

When we were ready to embark, everyone was surprised to hear me announce to John, "You'll be very careful won't you? You know I've never enjoyed being around water."

"Then, in Heaven's name whatever possessed you to contemplate coming on a six-day canoe trip?" he asked, exhibiting just a tad of annoyance.

"Well, whose idea was it?" I retorted.

From then on, I panicked every time he strayed more than twenty feet away from the shore which caused just a little more tension.

We rented wheels to transport our canoes along the portages, but the Davises had brought along their own wheels which were six inches too wide for the trails. Herb thought he was much too macho to rent wheels, so we had to wait for him at the end of each portage while he first carried his belongings on his back and then impressed us with his strength by running along the trail, topless, balancing his canoe on his head. As it turned out, it wasn't too much of an inconvenience to wait for him because Basil and Tish were fighting hard with each other and with the canoe, trying to keep it atop wheels that kept veering up the steep banks on either side of the trail.

Tricky to manoeuvre those wide wheels along the portages!

The second day, a storm came up, and the wind was blowing so hard that the rain was driving across horizontally. For some reason, Herb, who has always fancied himself as a born leader, took off across the middle of the lake and the Davises foolishly followed him. They were traumatised, believing their end had come; they have never forgotten the experience and talk about it to this day. We, along with John and Chris did our best to hug the shore, but the wind was so strong, it kept blowing us off towards the middle of the lake which terrified me and caused me to plead with John, even though he was doing his best against a strong gale.

All eight of us made it to the first camp site alive but like drowned rats and with all our belongings soaked through. An obviously experienced German tourist lit a fire while we erected our sopping wet tents and then strung lines between the trees in an attempt to dry out our gear while reminding ourselves that we were on holiday.

The weather perked up the next day, but there was the sound of discordant muttering emanating from each canoe as we paddled on. Several times, we found ourselves marooned atop logs in the water because the person in the bow was not paying attention and unable to shout, "Log ahead!" to the person paddling in the stern.

And now this, added to the embarrassment of Fagin!

One day, Tish seriously injured her leg while trying to climb out of her canoe to get onto the bank. She was bleeding badly and really needed to see a doctor, but Fagin was of little help—I believe he may have suggested that she would probably need to have the leg amputated. The reluctant ambulance attendant skulked in the background.

At the end of the trip, we all realised that canoeing with one's spouse is not to be recommended, and in future we would stick to other kinds of holidays which we have done very happily with all of the same people at different times.

Plain paddling from now on? Probably not!

Well, there was one other exception involving a camping trip with Penny and Herb in the Pyrenees. "One More Peak Herb," as he became known from then on, will not forget the day Penny screamed something shockingly obscene from her

They could all force a smile for the camera!

peak across to his above. Even Molly Bloom would have been embarrassed, and everyone from the Mediterranean to the Bay of Biscay would have been blushing that day. If Flo had been there, she could have given Penny a quick lesson on the rope trick.

At one point on that adventure, we pitched our tents for a three-day stay. Every night, I complained to John that I could feel something moving about underneath me, but his response was always, "Oh! I'm sure you're imagining it, just get to sleep and let everyone do the same." As we took down the tents on the fourth morning, we discovered a large toad or bullfrog which had been trapped beneath my restless form for three days but had managed to survive. There followed a humorous discussion about what would happen if I kissed it, but Penny and I winked at each other knowingly. We already had enough princes on this trip.

CHAPTER TWENTY-SIX

Without travel, our existence, our memories, our literature, our dreams, our everything would be very poor, very boring, very limited!

— Mehmet Murat ildan

SOME OF OUR FRIENDS prefer to travel in style and others like the Davises are much like us and prefer a mix of experiences. It is with them we have travelled to Peru, camped along the trail to Machu Picchu and stayed with families in a mountain village —Caccaccolla—in conditions much more primitive than my home in rural South Wales.

We went there as part of a tourist group whose mission it is to help out the less fortunate by paying the villagers to house tourists, to act as porters on the Inca Trail and to provide opportunities for them to sell their weavings and other artistic endeavours. While it was a wonderful experience for us, I questioned the real benefit to the local people. With the money they earn, they are changing their old ways of living that have sustained them for hundreds of years. Although the women were still cooking in cast iron pots over open fires on the floor in the corner of the room, almost every home seemed to have a television purchased with their new-found wealth. This is propelling them into the ways of the western world, and possibly causing them to make comparisons which can lead to dissatisfaction and have a negative impact on the culture.

Helena Norberg Hodge, to whom Greg Mortenson refers in "Three Cups of Tea" wrote about this very issue in her book, "Ancient Futures." She explains how the lives of the happy, self- sufficient people in Ladakh, Kashmir, were altered by the introduction of western ideas.

At the same time, we are making an effort to step back in time, recognising the folly of our ways that are destroying our earth, and trying to lead more sustainable lives.

To go or not to go? —that is the question!

The porters on our hike came from the surrounding villages, and we were in awe of their stamina. They ran in mountainous terrain with only bits of rubber tire for footwear, while carrying our heavy packs, and they would have tents, tables and chairs set up and a meal prepared for us as we arrived at the campsite completely knackered just from carrying our cameras.

Bas and Tish going native in Peru!

Porters leading us on the trek to Machu Picchu.

It was on this visit to Peru that we also continued on to Puno and took a trip to Amantani Island in the middle of Lake

Titicaca where we stayed with a local family.

We were greeted at the dock by our host who was probably close to our age but was so wrinkled and copper-skinned from the sun, as well as being generously layered in grime, that she could have been one hundred-years-old. We couldn't believe her level of fitness, however, as she tore off up the hill at the speed of light, carrying our bags, as we struggled to keep up, badly affected by the altitude and gasping for breath at every step. At 12,500 ft, Lake Titicaca is the highest navigable lake in the world.

After a light meal and a brief rest, we were dismayed to learn that we were then expected to trek to the temple ruins—Pachamama—Mother Earth, and Pachatata—Father Earth, at the top of the hill. Every step was a challenge, and we paused frequently to catch our breath while our hosts fed us coca leaves to ward off altitude sickness, before lightly skipping on ahead.

When we reached the ruins around sunset, we were instructed to walk around them three times and make a wish. We both wished for long life and health for ourselves and our family and friends, but at the same time, were having doubts that we would make it through the night.

Since all the inhabitants appeared to be so old yet so fit, I asked about their longevity and was told that the islanders often live to be in their eighties or nineties and even over one hundred-years-old. I then asked about disease, specifically cancer, and I learned it was rare. When I said that it was rampant in Canada, a gentleman who appeared never to have had a very close relationship with soap and water said, "Well your problem in North America is that you people wash too much!" I believe he may have a point!

The indigenous people on Amantani, who consider themselves to be direct descendants of the Incas, hold full title to their land, and at that time, were amongst few in the world to have avoided government control. They exist on fishing, and a cooperative farming system growing quinoa, potatoes and corn.

Unfortunately, they are now being exploited by tour companies which, while providing some level of economic independence, pose a threat to their self-determination.

The next day, we walked across Taquile Island and were taught about family customs. Married men, we were told, wear black and red hats, single men red and white hats, and men of class wear multicoloured ones. A man of class seemed to be a married man with three children. Finally, somewhere in the world, John had become a man of class.

Young people get together young—around 16 to 17 years. When a boy likes a girl, he throws stones at her, and if she likes him, they get together and move in with his parents. They must produce children before they marry, and if after five or six years there are no children, they must separate or leave the island. It all seems a little harsh.

Before we left the lake, we stopped off at the Uros Floating Islands. They rest on a thick bed of totora roots with reeds stacked on top and are anchored to stakes driven into the bottom of the lake. They can last as long as thirty years, and then a replacement can be built. The homes, the boats and the furniture are all intricately made from reeds. Unlike the other islands we had visited, they are so close to Puno on the mainland that they have become a tourist trap with not an ounce of authenticity remaining. When the natives waved us off singing "Twinkle, Twinkle Little Star," I began to think I was on a film set at Universal Studios and decided that we should be more selective about our travels in future.

That is why we found ourselves with the Davises, some years later, sleeping side by side on the floor of a monastery in Myanmar where the chanting of monks and the banging of gongs kept us awake most of the night. This was at the culmination of a luxury tour, led by our wonderful guides, Debbie, Robi and Daniel, and entailed a three-day walk through the Myanmar hills experiencing life as it really was in centuries past. I won't tell you what the luxury part dinged us, but the camping trip cost just $14.00 per day, including meals which were cooked by our two guides and eaten by candlelight in a monastery where gold-clad Buddhas kept vigil on every side.

Basil, contemplating a night on the floor in the monastery, Myanmar.

A centuries old tradition—winnowing in the Myanmar hills.

Our modest lodge on Inle Lake, Myanmar—the luxury stage.

The better-looking half of the Myanmar tour participants.

We crashed a wedding and were photographed with the bride and groom.

We were fortunate enough to visit Myanmar during what I believed was one of the rare peaceful periods, but we were not fully made aware of the dire situation in northern Rakhine State where those of the minority ethnic group were already being uprooted from their homeland. This practice has escalated since 2017, with hundreds of thousands of Rohingya Muslims being forcibly displaced and settled in the world's largest refugee camp in Cox's Bazar, Bangladesh, where despite huge support from Medecins Sans Frontieres, appalling living conditions are leading to hunger, disease and death.

Now, as I write, the military is disputing the results of the recent election of Aung San Suu Kyi and are attacking, incarcerating and killing civilian protesters, including children. It seems to be a never-ending tragedy and a shocking indictment of a world that doesn't give a damn.

The major news in the paper this morning, is about the killing of one police officer in the vehicle attack on the U.S. Capitol, and the world's shocked response to the tragedy. Meanwhile, I could find no report on the deaths of more than

550 peaceful protestors who are attempting to uphold the legitimacy of Myanmar's Democratic Government.

It makes me sad to think of a place of such beauty and history and above all, such hospitable people who still manage to maintain a welcoming spirit in a country that has seen so much turmoil.

Once in a while, we find ourselves with friends who are not accustomed to travelling rough, and I believe the Taylors may still be thawing out from their experience camping with us amongst the yaks in an alpine meadow at 12,000 ft above the Tiger's Nest in Bhutan. It was bitterly cold, and the sleeping bags provided were inadequate. I had been disparaged for toting my minus10 degree bag around India for the previous three weeks, anticipating the frigid temperatures, but I was feeling pretty snug—not to mention smug—as the rest of the crew became hypothermic during the night.

A nippy night at 12,000 ft —Paul checking the temperature in disbelief!

I think the Taylors, at that point, thought they had sunk as low as they could go, but they had yet to experience the promised, rejuvenating soak in "an herb-infused hot tub" which, in reality, was a type of wooden manger in a grubby, earthen-floored shed, filled with tepid water and a tangle of floating, green weeds.

In many ways, Bhutan was a disappointment. The country in the eastern Himalayas is beautiful and the people friendly and welcoming. Knowing that the country measures itself in terms of Gross National Happiness, we didn't expect to find the same social problems that we experience in the western world. Perhaps we were being naïve, but to learn that teenage pregnancy, alcohol and drug dependence, mental illness, crime and divorce are rampant was quite a shock. Our guide who was already on her third marriage, expressed amazement when she learned that we three couples had all been married for more than fifty years. She thought that sounded awfully boring!

We were also distressed to see many stray dogs hanging around the dzongs—monasteries—looking for food, and when I attempted to prevent a Buddhist monk from beating one of them half to death, I began to believe that I was witness to a sham and decided that I wouldn't become a Buddhist any time soon.

Having said that, we did enjoy the culture, and a visit to the Crane Festival, which celebrates the return of the black-necked cranes each year, was a highlight. We were excited to arrive during their migration from their breeding grounds in the upper Tibetan Plateau to the Phobjika Valley where they roost until spring. Buddhists believe that these four-foot-tall, majestic birds—related to the North American whooping crane—are messengers from heaven, conveying news of long-lost ancestors and loved ones and that they bring long life, peace and prosperity.

Another highlight for me was a visit to a primary school. There, we saw the children producing written work in English at a level that far outstrips the standard expected of my school-age grandchildren and would be quite an eye-opener for the B.C. Ministry of Education.

Over the course of two weeks, we visited many dzongs, each one seemingly more elaborate than the previous one. As we were coming down the steps of a particularly ornate one, I heard a voice shouting out, "Mrs. Dudley," and there was a former Collingwood student, Jessie Hussein, smiling up at me. It was such a pleasure to see Jessie who was treating her Thai nanny—a much-loved presence in her family for many years—to a trip to Bhutan en route to Thailand to visit her ageing mother. Coincidences don't only happen on El Camino, it would appear.

With Jessie at the Dzong

Visiting the dzongs in Bhutan is akin to visiting the castles in Wales. After a while they all look the same, or to quote my mother, "When you've seen one, you've seen 'em all," but because of the coincidence, that particular dzong is one that I remember more clearly, as well as the story that we were told about why it had been so elaborately built.

It was apparently ordered by the queen mother, to ward off the evils that would befall her son for being born in the year of the monkey. I thought it might have been more sensible and cheaper to have arranged to have her son born in a different year. We were not told if the enormous expense paid off.

We have been very fortunate to have travelled so extensively—and here I have only touched on a few of our trips—but we have never regretted for one moment spending time and money on the holidays we have taken and the educational experiences which have enriched our lives and the lives of our children. For me, those frequent holidays have also been a needed escape for me to replenish the soil that still clings to my roots, and to breathe new life into that broken-off piece of my heart I left behind in Britain.

Having had interesting projects to keep us engaged, and without any of the hardships that have been faced by so many, we have weathered the pandemic very well, and I have adjusted to the reality that I will not have my usual escape for a few years. If Covid-19 has taught us anything it is how adaptable we humans can be.

CHAPTER TWENTY-SEVEN

It's not how much money we make that ultimately makes us happy between nine and five. It's whether or not our work fulfills us.

— Malcolm Gladwell

IN THE FALL OF 1984, I was contacted by a friend, Linda, who asked me if I would be interested in a part-time tutoring position at Collingwood School where she had been employed since the previous September. She said that it would likely lead to a full-time job the following year. Having lost my teachers' aide job, I had been intending to return to teaching, so it was an auspicious call. I jumped at the opportunity.

Collingwood School is an Independent School in West Vancouver that was envisioned by a group of parents who saw a need for such a facility on the North Shore. Those who wanted private education for their children had, up until that point, been driving or bussing them over to Independent schools in Vancouver.

Laura Groos—the "First Founder" of the school was the driving force behind the idea and the name came from a Flower-class Corvette—HMCS Collingwood, that had served with the Royal Canadian Navy during WW11 and on which her father, David Groos, had served as Commander in 1942. David

Mackenzie, who had served in the British Navy and was also an ardent rugby fan, became the first Headmaster, and Nick Geer, another Founding member, became the first Chairman of the Board. Nick tragically died in an automobile accident in California, and his Celebration of Life was a fitting tribute to the calibre of parent who had realised that vision and coined the school's motto: Ex Visu Ad Verum—From Vison to Reality.

I wondered about the wisdom of naming a school after a ship, and those of us who were at Collingwood from the beginning felt certain it was destined to sink in rough seas. Violent storms and gales rocked the ship intermittently, and some members of the crew were tossed overboard or jumped within the first few years. We were almost grounded by rocks on more than one occasion. Miraculously, several threatened mutinies were avoided, but the captain had to be thrown a life belt more than once. Rumblings under the surface continued for some time, but we eventually navigated the ship into calmer waters, dodging a Lusitania-like fate.

The school opened in the old Glenmore School, in West Vancouver, which had closed due to declining numbers. I don't think anyone had quite realised how much interest there would be in the new school, so it was a Herculean effort to find enough staff, furniture and supplies to open the school in time for the new school year.

I became a full-time teacher there in 1985. At my interview with Mr. Mackenzie, I admitted to knowing nothing about rugby, even though I was Welsh, but I had the right accent, so I was acceptable. I was offered a paltry salary and when the contract was drawn up, the amount had been reduced by a further $1,000, but I was so delighted to get the job that I did not question it.

When I first entered my Grade Two classroom, it was bare of supplies except for a mishmash of old-fashioned desks that had been discarded by a Squamish school. I believe there were many parents who must have been wondering what they had signed up for. John quickly got to work making furniture for me; he made tables out of our old decking, painted the legs and covered the tops with yellow and blue Formica—the school colours. Throughout August, he made shelving, book cases and notice boards, and Colin and Marie donated their comfortable old couch. By the time the children arrived in September, the room was transformed.

Perusing the history of those early years, I was amused to read, "Some were not prepared for the threadbare challenge they encountered, but many of them—notably Lore Acton, Diana Bedford, Kathleen Culham, Sandra Dawson, Rose Dudley, Roger Hatch, Kathy Turner and others would power through and become venerable pillars of the institution."

I enjoyed my work, and I loved the school. The children were delightful and the parents enthusiastic and determined to do their best to ensure the school's success. Just as the tragedies in Lions Bay had built a strong community, the initial choppy waters at the school united the staff. I had worked in other schools with wonderful colleagues, but right from the beginning, there was a special atmosphere at Collingwood.

My first Grade Two class at Collingwood.

The only fly in the ointment was the number of meetings that were held and the countless committees that were formed to solve initial problems. We had meetings just to arrange future meetings, others to analyse past meetings, more to establish committees, and committees to arrange more meetings—sheer madness!

I couldn't hazard a guess at the number of meetings that were held to determine a Mission Statement—the fad for organisations in the early eighties. John had also been subjected to that fad. He had a name for it—pretentious crap. Those meetings went on for hours, days, weeks and months—maybe years. I wonder how many people in the world felt they were being held hostage, engulfed by pie-charts, wads of paper on chart holders and huddles of people brain-storming to frame ideas for a never-ending process? When I think of storming, I think—assault—attack—onslaught, which is what I felt my brain had undergone following every one of those meetings, temporary recovery coming only with a generous shot of sherry in the bathtub. Other members of staff dealt with the assault in any way they saw fit. The music teacher, Robert, slept peacefully through most of the meetings, only waking with a start and bringing us all back into the present, when he fell off his chair.

I was at the school for sixteen years, but I can't remember if we ever succeeded in our quest. If we did, I do not have the faintest idea, to this day, what the Mission Statement is. My only mission was to be allowed to do the work for which I had been hired, and I suspect millions of employees around the world felt exactly the same. What a complete waste of man hours!

I wonder if my former students who will now be in their thirties and forties, and possibly parents and teachers themselves, will remember some of the projects that we undertook together—the great newspaper bridge project, for example, in which John was involved with them in building a 16 ft-long replica of the Lions Gate Bridge, and they were challenged to build newspaper bridges capable of supporting their own weight. Then there were annual class plays, and the whole Primary School extravaganzas directed by Mandy, the talented head of the Primary School—all great fun!

One experience that no one could possibly forget was the Grade One chicken-hatching fiasco. To see those little balls of fluff pecking their way out of their shells was so rewarding, but

Was this Christmas or Hallowe'en? The witches of Collingwood.

I had not given any thought to how we would find homes for them later on.

We didn't succeed until they had grown big enough to escape from their pen and perch all over the classroom—It's a mystery why someone didn't call the Vancouver Health Department. One morning, the janitor, who was no fan of the project, became exceedingly agitated when he found them clucking down the hallway. Madame Turner, the French teacher, reached the point of refusing to enter the room because she said it smelled like a farm-yard. Our pets had become laying hens before we eventually found a suitable home for them on Vancouver Island.

Another annual project, one into which John found himself being dragged, was the building of the floats for the annual West Vancouver Community Day Parade—from revolving Ferris wheels to fairy castles and an anniversary cake

Just two of the floats that John and his crew of parents built for the West Vancouver Parade.

accompanied by 75 students in hard plastic tube candles which were almost impossible to walk in.

As a staff, one unforgettable, team-building event in which we participated for years was the annual 24-hour-relay which raised funds for the children's hospital.

Collingwood's fundraising team for the 24-hour-relay

As I had found the case to be at Talmud Torah, the parents and teachers had high expectations of the children. One of the most enjoyable and impressive school events was the annual Speech Competition in which all children from Grade One onwards were expected to participate. What a boost to a child's confidence!

At the end of my first year, the Board of Governors suggested a talent contest to determine how the teachers and board members could perform under such pressure—speeches, poetry readings, skits and the like. Many of the staff grumbled that it was the last thing that they wished to do on top of the extra end-of-term responsibilities, but John and I, always up for a challenge, wrote a satirical poem with 26 verses chronicling my experiences.

I needed a little Dutch courage to deliver it, so Madame Turner stood by, refilling my wine glass and egging me on. When I came upon that poem recently, I was reassured that my memory is sound. Following are just two verses:

Now I should say a bit about organisation,
It's the cause of the bulk of Di Bedford's vexation.
We hold meetings here with such skill and precision
But rarely, if ever, reach a decision.

When it comes to committees, well then there's no lack,
We have more in this school than a person can hack.
"Did you have a question?" Up goes a shout,
"Let's form a committee, let's sort this thing out."

I have been retired from the school for 20 years, but I still appreciate my connection and enjoy the retirement parties, anniversaries and special events to which former staff are invited. My last visit there was for a ceremony called, "Bringing Down the House," before the last building project would necessitate the destruction of the original Glenmore School. I was able to take a last look into my old classroom and immerse myself in the memories.

My last two years were spent at the new Junior School campus which was completed in 1999. Both Di and I were interested in working only half-time and the head, Graham, who was very amenable to the idea, created a job for us. He gave us the label, "Consultant," but that was a loose term for "General Dog's Body." It suited Di, because she still had young children, but I was bored out of my mind. I asked to go back to the classroom the following year which put Di out of work, but she didn't complain—not much!

In my last year, I went out on a high, having worked with a wonderful group of young colleagues under the leadership of a capable and professional head, Muir, who recognised that, "Leadership is not about who's boss or who's in charge, it's about who gains respect from others." I don't know who originally penned those words, but I know that all teachers who were lucky enough to have him as a boss would agree with the statement. I was also fortunate to end with a class of talented

My last Grade Three class—still at an age when they love their teacher!

Imagine!—Mr. Meredith was still skating at his advanced age!

Grade Three students who were real characters. Looking through the Collingwood Facebook page I came across one of them—Alexander, who is currently appearing in "Vikings." I always knew he was destined for stardom, and surely I'm allowed to take a little credit for what he has become!

Over the years, the school has gone from strength to strength and is recognised as one of the top schools in the country. Seeing the state-of-the-art buildings that now exist, it is difficult to remember how spartan the conditions were in those first few years. It is testament to a group of people who wanted the best for their children, had faith that they could pull it off and were willing to put their effort and money behind it. I feel very privileged to have been part of the Collingwood family and one of those "venerable pillars of the institution." even though the description made me feel like an ancient columnar stanchion.

A group of former teachers, soon to be in their eighties, still enjoy getting together for lunches and afternoon teas. We call ourselves the FMNs—the Forget-Me-Nots. Most of the

The year that four of the FMNs earned their gold cards.

discussions reflect on our years at Collingwood, and I sense that my old colleagues also cherish the memories.

I believe there are far too many people who have stuck it out in jobs that they don't really enjoy. In my generation, a change of career was rare and even frowned upon. How discouraging it must have been to know that the only light at the end of the tunnel was retirement after forty years or so. In

Collingwood ladies dressed for a Dudley wedding.

The staff grew exponentially, from 16 in 1984 to a ratio of 1 staff member to 1.8 students today.

my working life, I learned the difference between a job that I enjoyed and one where I was just putting in time.

It is interesting to observe the working life experiences of our children. Most of them have had job changes over the years except our youngest daughter, Nicola, who considers that she has a dream job with the airlines—and who wouldn't love to lie on Mexican and Caribbean beaches or stroll around European capitals and buy out Marks and Spencer in London while your husband is caring for the children and holding the fort back home? That is the dream part which allows her to forget the number of demanding passengers who can quickly turn that dream into a nightmare. The pandemic has put her out of work, she hopes temporarily. She can't imagine losing a job she loves. She doesn't envy her sisters who have highly paid but stressful government jobs.

"The life of Riley." Nicola and Krista recovering from a gruelling five-hour flight.

We thought our son-in-law, Eric, was a little crazy to give up a successful engineering career to start his own business making health food bars, but he was bored with his job and knew when it was time to make the move—well, I suppose it does help that he has a working wife with a generous government pension which allows him to follow his dream. Wyatt gave up a lucrative position with an international software company because it took him away from home too frequently, and Marcel is hardly making use of his Political Science degree in the mountain bike industry, but they all feel that they have fulfilling careers.

Perhaps the winner in all of this is John who chose a career that allowed him lots of leisure time. Certainly, he suffered in silence for the first few years, but once he left the sea for the company office where he worked only alternate weeks, he was able to maintain a very balanced life.

Our children appreciate that he has been very much a part of their lives; he has been there for every birthday celebration, to attend their school concerts and graduations, to assist them with school projects and to be with them on extended vacations. John would agree with the following words that are attributed to Rabbi, Harold Kushner:

"No one on his death bed ever said, "I wish I'd spent more time at the office."

CHAPTER TWENTY-EIGHT

Passion in life IS life. It's contagious. Get naked and roll around in it. People who enjoy living have it all figured out. They are passionate, driven, alive, and they are real.

— Lorii Myers

EVERYONE WHO MEETS JOHN recognises that he epitomises the above description, although, as far as I know, they have yet to see him literally rolling around naked, and it might be best if they never get the opportunity. He is passionate about everything he undertakes, but his passion for trail building has been extraordinary. Many of the people who have helped him, over the years, would agree that his love of what he does is contagious.

When we returned to Lions Bay after our unplanned years away, it bothered him that there were no places to walk except on the streets. In his diary, I read that he had woken up at 3 a.m. on June 20th, 1999 and recalled a quote by Ralph Waldo Emmerson that he had seen that very day in the paper, "Don't go where the path may lead. Go instead where there is no path and leave a trail." That was all the motivation he needed to begin to change the situation.

Originally, he thought of building a trail between Lions Bay and Horseshoe Bay to join up with the Trans-Canada Trail, but because of watersheds that had to be crossed, he decided it was wiser to carve a circular trail that could be enjoyed by the village residents.

The work on the first trail—"The Totally Unnecessary Trail"— now renamed "The Erin Moore Trail," in memory of the little girl who was killed on it by a falling boulder—began in December of that year, and by January, John had enlisted the help of another couple—Rudy and Trudi Luethy. He was still employed at the time, but working only alternate weeks allowed him to spend two weeks of every month doing what he loved. I helped during my holidays and became part of the team as soon as I retired in 2001. I cannot honestly say that I completely embrace his passion, rather the love of his passion. Being a country girl who thrives on wide open skies and green fields, a rainforest is not my preferred milieu, but I enjoy the physical challenge, the camaraderie and an activity that benefits others.

With regular help from yet another enthusiastic couple, Richard and Pat Grass, and the occasional assistance of others, that first trail would take seven years to complete. By that time, all the trail-blazers were well into their sixties, and when one considers the heavy equipment, including a chainsaw, that had to be carried to the work site—sometimes an hour's walk away — it was an incredible achievement. The first part of the trail, up to the view point, was officially opened in June of that same year and was attended by 28 people between the ages of two and sixty-seven years, and since then it has been enjoyed by thousands.

Once John had begun, there was no stopping him, and at the age of 78, he is still following his passion. Many of the trails are challenging even to walk so were verging on the impossible to build. On one particularly steep one, the members of the crew began to balk about what they saw as a dangerous situation. They complained that they were having sleepless nights, and that's how that particular trail became "The Sleepless Nights' Trail."

The Luethys and John celebrating the completion of the first half of the Erin Moore Trail.

The Grasses, along with Brian, still at it in 2021!

The most popular trail is still the easy, relatively flat one, "The Centennial Trail," which links Lions Bay and Brunswick

Celebrating the completion of the Erin Moore Trail--2007

Rob—one of those younger regulars soon to have a buggered-up body.

Beach and was opened with great fanfare, including young musicians performing in the forest and a barbecue at the end, in May 2011. We are about to celebrate its tenth anniversary.

Over the years, John has conned many more people into helping him. With increased technology, he no longer has to beg people over the phone as he used to do when looking for volunteers to help. He remembers when he was building the school playscape over 40 years ago, that frequently a wife would answer the phone, and he would hear an agitated husband whispering, "Tell him I'm not home." Now with email, they can't escape, so he grabs them as soon as they retire, before their knees hips and backs have given out. Of course, it doesn't take too many years of trail building for their bodies to get buggered up completely.

I am always readily available, so when trails have to be built, they have to be built regardless of the day. A new source of free re-bar or a donation of wood sends John into paroxysms of ecstasy, and they have to be put to good use without delay. That's much more important to him than a mere wedding anniversary celebration.

Our 38th wedding anniversary. Who said, "Romance is dead?"

It won't surprise anyone to learn that John has expressed a desire, when he dies, to have his ashes scattered somewhere in the forest. Since I would like us to remain together in death—and I assume that he would opt for the same arrangement—I have yet to break the news to him that it his turn to compromise, so he will be emigrating in a small urn.

All those neighbours who he has conned into helping him over the years, will be in agreement when he says, "There is nothing more satisfying or invigorating than engaging in physical labour with a like-minded group of people, to achieve something that will be of benefit to others." That, of course, is the reason why we will all keep answering the call.

He does tend to have a very persuasive nature, and one of his most impressive acquisitions for the Centennial Trail was a metal bridge donated by the Ministry of Transport. For that, he earned the honour of having his name mounted on it in perpetuity. He was a lot luckier than poor old Frank who didn't get his name displayed on a shed until after he'd popped his clogs.

Only John could have talked the Ministry of Transport into donating something of this magnitude.

Once the trails were built, John formed a hiking group. It had originally been started by a small group of "Project Hands" ladies, but his input was requested, and it was not long before he had taken over the responsibility. He sends out the information every Friday accompanied by inspiring quotes. He has about 220 people on the hiking list of whom a maximum of 25 ever turn up, but people tell him to keep them on the list just to receive the quotes. I have been impressed with his tenacity during the Covid-19 pandemic. Although we can no longer hike together, he has continued to send out the weekly bulletins including relevant quotes.

John has always loved Bob Dylan's lyrics for the messages they convey, and this excerpt from the song, Forever Young, seems to have words that John lives by.

> May your hands always be busy
> May your feet always be swift
> May you have a strong foundation
> When the winds of changes shift
> May your heart always be joyful
> May your song always be sung
> And may you stay forever young.

We have had some interesting times on our hikes, and, as a leader, he has found the ladies particularly difficult to lead. They tend to talk too much and not pay attention to the directions or where they are going. From ladies getting lost and confronting bears to those who scaled the side of a bluff, he has found it necessary to call "Search and Rescue" on several occasions. Most people now know that his hikes are never going to be a walk in the park.

We can't, however, blame John for the near tragedy in the third picture below. He wasn't leading this overnight camping trip up to Diamond Head, but if John Mingay had not been with us, Max would have been a goner! I wonder if Max has ever rewarded John for saving his life when he was choking to death?

How did she get stuck up there?

A bee sting led to the ride of her life!

Rose Dudley

Max, re-enacting his close call with death.

CHAPTER TWENTY-NINE

Friends in your life are like the pillars on your porch. Sometimes, they hold you up, and sometimes they lean on you —sometimes, it's just enough to know they're standing by.

— Elizabeth Foley

IT WAS A HUGE decision by John to move us to another country and never one I would have made independently, but following our arrival, it was the very smallest of decisions that we made together that has largely shaped our lives here.

I mentioned earlier that a friend in England had given us an address of an English couple living in the West End. What I did not say was that if it had been up to John, we may never have contacted them. He, being a rather reserved English gentleman, decided that we shouldn't impose on them, but as you already know, we knocked on their door and they welcomed us with open arms. They, Colin and Marie Moores, who became Aunty Marie and Uncle Colin to our children as we became Aunty Rose and Uncle John to theirs, will be surprised, as will others, to know that with the exception of my colleagues at Collingwood School, an office buddy of John's who has clothed him for years with his cast-offs, and good friends who are members of the Seniors' Cycle Group, all our oldest friends can be traced back to Colin and Marie. One can only speculate on what a different path our lives might have taken if we had decided not to visit them that night.

All of our friends in West Vancouver can be traceable to them, and since it was Colin who invited John to hike the Lions two days before I flew to England—and you've already heard the disturbing details of that little drama—then we can say that he is also the reason that we have lived such a full life and made so many friends here in Lions Bay.

Just the other night, I thought about the part Colin and Marie have played in our lives, when we were enjoying our Book Club meeting on Zoom. There were eleven members of our Book Club family there all linked to Colin. I smiled to myself when I scanned the group and realised that, with a few exceptions, I could refer to them as our stock-broker family. Colin had been in the investment business. He is now married to Holly and Marie to Roger, but they all get along famously.

Over the years, we have made so many new friends in Lions Bay, mainly through activities, some of which we have instigated ourselves, and we have also taken vacations with some of those people. There are too many to mention individually, but it would be remiss of me not to pay tribute to our volunteer gardening group—now temporarily disbanded, our hiking group, the trail-building team, our tennis and badminton buddies, and the ladies boot camp which is presently on hold. My two book clubs' participants have had to meet on Zoom during the pandemic. Even our annual New Year's Eve revellers were reduced to meeting on Zoom this year, but although we were somewhat averse to the idea initially —being mostly old fogies—we enthusiastically embraced the idea of meeting in our pyjamas—at least those of us who wear them—and being in bed well before midnight.

We have been privileged to be hosted for years by the Wrays—another culinary team who can knock Martha Stewart's socks off —but we may well have started a new trend. At our age, we are all enjoying not having to clean ourselves up to go out. One more year of this way of life and I believe John and I will become contented recluses.

The Sun Run training team which began in 2011 with 19 participants, has now dwindled to seven or eight hard-core types. Sadly, we will be missing the race for the second year in a row because of the pandemic, but I intend to be back on the start line with the team in 2022, as long as my pain-free, 80-year-old knees keep holding me in good stead.

Members of the Volunteer Gardening Group.

Sam really knows how to water.

All of these experiences and the people we have met along the way have greatly enriched our lives, and we feel fortunate to have met them. In the words of Helen Keller:
"My friends have made the story of my life."

Is this a book club or a gourmet dining club?

It looks far more like a gourmet dining club!

A birthday surprise!

The hike list went out to 220, but only 14 showed up!

Hike to Joffre Lakes, and only 12 showed up!

Rose Dudley

The Rainforest Ramblers trained hard to become the Rainforest Racers for the 10 km Sun Run.

John didn't seem too excited about the men winning the bocce trophy.

He Promised Me Roses, But I Forgot They Have Thorns.

Our Book Club that has been in existence for over thirty years.

A creative New Year's Eve party, thanks, again, to the Wrays. Covid -19 turned us from Boomers to Zoomers

    To the concern of many of our friends, John has never had much faith in doctors and has not seen one for the last 28 years. He believes that the body is much like a smoothly-running car, but if you take it into the garage, the mechanics will always find something wrong with it, and then you will be forced to get it fixed at great expense. In the case of one's body, the fixing, he believes will probably kill you. Many people are aghast at this philosophy, but our friend, John G, is one person who is not at all fazed by such a belief. I have heard him say many times, "Never trust a doctor." Well, he should know! He rightly points out that not one of us is going to get out of here alive. My husband has always said, "If they tell me I am going to die tomorrow, I won't welcome the news, but I can honestly say that to have been blessed with such a wonderful family, to have been surrounded by friends who really have been the pillars on my porch, and not to have experienced one moment of boredom or a day without laughter in my 78 years, I have had one hell of a charmed life." Of course, I believe that his "hell of a charmed life" has had much to do with him being fortunate enough to have married a toughened up, country girl like me.

EPILOGUE

Compromise and sacrifice are the hardest things to pursue. You will find true love for someone special the day you, without a thought, go for the above two.

— Kumar Aakash

PEOPLE WHO HAVE WRITTEN about their lives are inevitably asked the same question, "Why did you decide to write a memoir?—did you find it cathartic?" I would have to say that I write only with the intention of producing a historical record for my children, grandchildren and the generations that will follow. This narrative, however, has also, in the writing, become a tribute to my family and to all my Canadian friends who have added so much joy to my life.

I will admit that this book has also been written with a desire to let people know how miserable my life was on my arrival in Canada and how homesick I was, and I know that there are so many immigrants who will be able to identify with my early experiences and my feelings today. I also wish people to realize that often what they see on the surface— a charmed life to them—a wonderful marriage, a close-knit family, success and fulfilment, and friends everywhere—is often concealed under a veil. I wanted to open a window into what sacrifice for love means. Anyone who has lived a life that was chosen for them by someone else will be able to relate.

In writing this memoir, I have exposed my innermost thoughts, and, undoubtedly, some of my friends will express surprise or even think of me as ungrateful, when they consider how fortunate I have been to live such a full life, but regret for the past does not preclude happiness in the present. My family and friends see, and I recognise, that I have had a wonderful life here in my adopted country, but it did not come without sacrifice, and in the telling—particularly of those early years—I have been reliving a painful past.

At the moment, during the pandemic, we are separated from the lives of our family and friends and disconnected from our normal way of living. We are stuck in the present with an uncertain future which is possibly what makes the memories of the past more vivid and the desire to chronicle them even more pressing.

We all have thoughts that we choose to conceal, but we delude ourselves if we think we can erase normal reactions to our experiences. My memories of a lonely and miserable past haven't prevented me from enjoying life to the full or recognising that Canada is one of the greatest places in the world in which to live. I have chosen to bring my feelings into the light, because I believe we all need to be true to ourselves.

Perhaps, my suffering in the early years was more a figment of my imagination than the reality of the situation at the time, or I have been determined to compete with Tish and Chris for supremacy in the misery stakes. As a gentleman by the name of Edward St. Aubyn once said, "People never remember happiness with the same care that they lavish on preserving every detail of their suffering." I think we can all concur with the wisdom of Mr. St. Aubyn.

Yes, there is no doubt that my first years in Canada were tough, but tough compared to what? I think of the Syrian refugee families who have been sponsored over the last few years—several by my daughters and their friends and neighbours in Lions Bay—and it should put things into perspective. We did not come from a war-torn land, we didn't have to pray every single day, as they do, for parents and siblings to be spared from the next bomb that might drop on their refugee camp, we spoke the language of our adopted country—almost—and we had a basic knowledge of the system. Their lives will continue to be a struggle until they get fully established, but all I see in their eyes and their hearts is gratitude for the opportunity they have been given to live in a safe and democratic country like Canada.

How can I compare a short period of loneliness and a longing for my country of birth to the Wade family's devastating loss of two teenaged sons in the Alberta Creek landslide or the Moores' loss of their seven-year-old daughter in a rock-fall? How does a man ever recover from seeing his pregnant wife washed over a bridge and out into Howe Sound?

What right do I or any of us have to complain about a little loneliness in life or sacrifices we have had to make, when we are aware of all the atrocities that have occurred throughout history and are still occurring every day around the world—man's inhumanity to man?

How can we justify whining about what may seem like trivialities when so many people including children go hungry every day and have no place to live except the street, even in Vancouver—a wealthy city which is considered to be one of the best places to live in the world?

Today, I think of all those who have had their lives cut short through disease or tragedy, unfortunate people who are presently sick and dying and those who have lost loved ones in the Covid-19 pandemic which is sweeping the world as I write.

But the misery and misfortunes of others never mitigate what one might have endured; a comparison is of naught to personal suffering. I did tend to dwell on my unhappiness at the beginning of my story attributing it to being removed, by the choice of another person, from what I still think of as home. Will I always miss my country of birth? I can honestly say that while my life following the first few miserable years has been happy, the answer is yes, I still miss aspects of Britain every single day— wide-open skies and expansive green fields, flower-filled country lanes, the intoxicating scent of bluebell woods, new-born lambs, the cuckoo's call, the smell of new-mown hay, the taste of Welsh new potatoes and tomatoes, picturesque villages—all those things and more that are stamped for ever on my childhood senses and cannot, should not and will never be erased.

A woodland path, full of light, on the Pembrokeshire Coast Trail—South Wales

The following poem by A.E Housman, sent to me by Chris, beautifully expresses those feelings of nostalgia:

> Into my heart an air that kills
> From yon far country blows:
> What are those blue remembered hills?
> What spires, what farms are those?
> That is the land of lost content,
> I see it shining plain,
> The happy highways where I went
> And cannot come again.

On our long-distance walks in England with Chris and John G, we have had so many conversations about our husbands' decision to move to Canada as opposed to living our lives in Britain. As we trudged through bluebell woods, breathing in their exhilarating scent on the South West Coast Path, I remember asking John G what he would have done if Chris had refused to go along with him? Similarly, I asked him what did he think my husband would have done if I had rejected his plan? He couldn't answer. There weren't answers; they were purely hypothetical questions. It's impossible to know how things might have turned out if our lives had taken a different path.

All four of us love the same things about Britain and recognise that we are fortunate to have the opportunity to enjoy the best of both worlds. We have the means to visit the "Old Country" as often as it suits us, reconnect with all our oldest friends and immerse ourselves in the things we miss, while still appreciating that we have a fulfilling life in Canada. Despite that, there will always be that feeling of regret that no amount of time can wash away for we three women.

I became aware that this was still the case for Tish while we were enjoying dinner with her and Basil, only a few years ago, on our trip to India and Bhutan. As usual, the subject of our early lives in Britain and South Africa reared its ugly head. It began with me retelling the story of John selling the house while I was in Wales—the one that has given me much more mileage than the Zenith Circle of Sound record player. Surprisingly, they had never heard it before. That led from one story of lamentation to another until Tish suddenly threw her serviette down on the table with resolve declaring, "I don't want to talk about this anymore, it upsets me, and then I can't get to sleep."

As I was coming to the end of my story, I asked both my friends to send their thoughts on their initial experiences on their arrival in Canada, and how they feel today, and I am including them here so that you will be able to judge for yourselves who got the rawest deal. Tish said:

"That it took me sixteen years to become a citizen of Canada is a good indication as to my reluctance to accept my fate. Arriving pregnant, and with two little girls and a blissfully happy but unrealistic husband, it took me only hours to realise that the expectations I'd had of this fun, new adventure were but a dream. From furniture built by my engineer husband from two by fours and plywood which was practical but aesthetically a big fat zero, to clothing for us all from the thrift stores and household goods from Woodward's $1.49 days, to renovating houses around ourselves and four young children, those early years became a total blur.

The day our four children collectively thanked us for taking on the challenges of immigrating to a new country, was the day I realised that it HAD been worth it. The children have all had the opportunity to visit and work in South Africa and loved the country but have appreciated the safety, security, and opportunities that Canada has offered them. So, "Get over it, Mum!"

And Chris said:

"Job satisfaction and better prospects for my husband's career as a family doctor had so far been elusive, so in 1968 we left England for Canada. In fact, we left England for Canada three times on that same quest!

Flying across the Atlantic, five months pregnant with our thirteen-month-old daughter in tow, I felt a sense of promise in the air, but this mood rapidly faded as we arrived in a gloomy, depressed coal-mining town in Cape Breton.

That first night, a flickering light in our bedroom turned out to be the blazing house next door seemingly lit by a well-known pyromaniac. Our friendly landlord was not only the town policeman but also a chronic alcoholic.

As I took my daily walks with my toddler trying to process my 'good fortune' I had to keep a sharp eye out for snarling dogs which had taken a fancy to my increasingly swelling ankles. I couldn't help noticing that those dogs seemed to be just as dispirited as the people, and so many of them were missing a leg. That early optimism had quickly dissipated. All I yearned for was the bucolic landscape and the sophistication of the country I had left behind.

We did go back to England only to return in 1970 to the same Nova Scotian town. This time, I was six months pregnant with two small daughters in tow and a strong sense of déjà vu! The arrival of a new baby did little to raise my spirits.

Long story short, and once more back in England, my peripatetic husband finally came to his senses. He applied to U.B.C. in Vancouver for a residency in anaesthesia—a great idea! By this time, I was in desperate need of some laughing gas!

And so, the crazy, 'neither here nor there' chapter in my life came to a close. The children started school and John was finally happy in his work. I opened my eyes and saw that all I needed to do now was embrace the challenges and finally settle down. The longed-for English landscape was replaced—almost —by the grandeur of the local mountains and the dramatic ocean views. This time there really was promise in the air."

Chris doesn't mention the story of a patient hammering on their door looking for urgent medical attention while John was ironing in his underwear wearing Wellington boots to prevent himself from being electrocuted by a malfunctioning iron. I was never told if he answered the door in that state, but if he did, in a town like she describes, I doubt the patient would have batted an eyelid.

My husband has been rather nervous about what I would write in this volume of my memoir. He has been warning everyone, ahead of time, that he didn't think he would be portrayed in the best possible light. He was threatening to write a rebuttal, even before reading what I have written. He was aware that I would point out that young men can be selfish, and he automatically assumed that the stories of the imported heavy book and record collection, the expensive record player and the selling of the house in my absence would be front and centre.

He knows full well, and he will not be surprised to see it written here, in black and white, that a piece of my heart was left behind in Britain. Whenever the subject comes up, he tends to ignore it, tell me to get over it or laugh it off. He still doesn't want to admit that I chose to sacrifice something that mattered to me a great deal, to give something that mattered more to him.

On the fiftieth anniversary of our arrival in Canada we asked our guests to wear blue to exemplify how I felt on that day. John gave a humorous speech, quoting from the last line of my first memoir, "I was seized with a sense of doom." He joked to the crowd about me taking fifty years to "get over it." but he knows, deep down, that I will never "get over it."

Someone once said, "It is not hard to make sacrifices for someone you love. The difficulty lies in finding that someone who is worth the sacrifice." Well, I was fortunate enough to find that someone. In my first memoir I said that he makes me laugh every day, and he is still making me laugh. I believe he will manage to make me laugh on his deathbed. He is a saint, highly thought of and loved by everyone.

I must have told Joyce—my potential 85-year-old Gran Fondo buddy, who gave me some sage advice in my first memoir—that since I did not have the crazy grandmother who had provided the humour in my first memoir, I would have to make John the butt of my jokes in this book. That's why, perhaps, she was concerned about what I might say, and felt she needed to remind me that, "He is a good guy, so I should always treat him with respect." She didn't need to worry.

I have never let on to him that every time I secretly look across the room at that balding old man of 78 reading, or rather sleeping with another "absolutely fascinating book" on his chest, I still see that handsome, sun-tanned, twenty-one-year-old with whom I fell in love on that camp-site almost 60 years ago. He has been well worth the sacrifice and we both know it.

So, things did have a way of working out, even though it wasn't my personal plan, but do you think that Chris, Tish and I will ever stop reminding our wonderful, tolerant husbands that we women were the ones who had to make the sacrifice for it to work out as splendidly as it has? Not a chance! That's just the way we women are.

Fifty years of happiness with a touch of blue.

A true blue day—July 23rd, 2017

In gratitude for a wonderful family—Celebrating our 50th Wedding Anniversary in Puerto Vallarta, 2017

ABOUT THE AUTHOR

Rose Dudley grew up on a farm in rural South Wales, during and after WW11, and from the age of four she attended a two-room village school where she was one of only 11 students. She still believes it was the place where she received the most important years of her education.

Following seven years in a prestigious high school in Monmouth, she completed her teacher training at Barrow Court in Somerset and taught in infants' schools in Bristol and Amersham, England, before emigrating to Canada with her husband, John, in 1967.

Since 1972, she and John have lived on the shores of Howe Sound in the picturesque village of Lions Bay, British Columbia. They have three married daughters and seven grandchildren.

This is Rose's second memoir which describes her life as a new immigrant and her difficult adjustment to a new country.

Her first book, "Memoir of a Sloppy, Spineless Creature" chronicles the challenges of growing up as a child of divorced parents, being raised by an abusive grandmother in a dysfunctional family, and the detrimental effects of the British class system.

SOME OF THE SPECIAL MOMENTS IN OUR LIVES

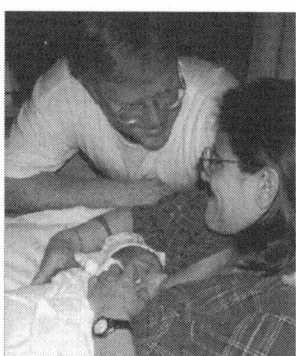

Helen and Wyatt's wedding, 1994 and first grandchild, Amanda, 1999

Retirements: Rose, 2001 and John, 2007

Weddings: Nicola and Marcel, 2002 and Alison and Eric, 2003

Practice hike for Eric's 4,265-km-walk on the Pacific Crest Trail, 2002 and after 3218 km on the trail, in California

Citizen of 2008 raising the flag for the 2009 Citizen

Rose's Floral Olympic Rings and Citizen of the Year, 2010

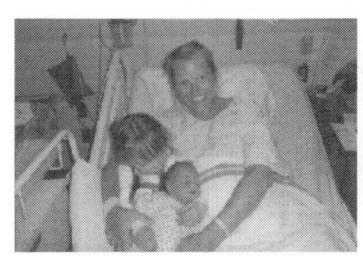

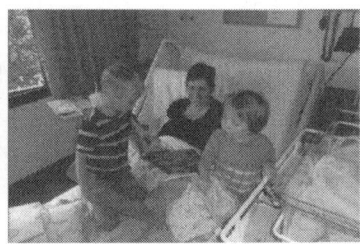

Last two grandchildren, Sienna and Sacha, 2012

The birth of the last two babies in 2012 completed our family.

45/75-years, Grand Fondo, Whistler, 2016

Covid-19 garden extension, Spring 2020

Thanksgiving dinner 2020 delivery in the time of Covid-19.

80th birthday tennis match 2021

ACKNOWLEDGEMENTS

I would like to thank my daughter, Nicola, and my husband, John, for their photo scanning skills and their patience in copying, and recopying again and again, copies that mysteriously "disappeared" or did not meet my high expectations. John also deserves extra thanks for his technological support, not to mention his emotional support on the day the whole manuscript vanished without a trace.

My friend's daughter, Holly Bedford, did a superb job of proof-reading. I am in awe of her eagle-eyed talent, and I wish to let her know that I will never forget how to spell "coyote" from now on. Should there be errors where I have added a few more paragraphs to the manuscript since she completed her task, I take full responsibility. I would also like to thank Holly for reassuring me that the story had merit when some of my family members were less than encouraging.

My granddaughter, Amanda Wyatt, formatted the manuscript using layouts supplied by Andrew Wray who was responsible for formatting my last memoir, "Memoir of a Sloppy, Spineless Creature," and she—as he had—did an excellent job. I cannot thank them enough.

I am indebted to Jenny Givner, at Acapella Book Design—acapellabookcoverdesign@gmail.com for creating the cover. I recommend her highly for her artistic talent as well as her expedition of a project, not to mention her patience.

The photograph of Ray Saunders, on Page 85, is republished with the express permission of the Vancouver Sun, a division of Postmedia Network Inc.

Lastly, I would like to thank my husband and family, and a host of wonderful friends—many of whom will find themselves amongst these pages—for providing me with a life filled with adventure, love and laughter.

Manufactured by Amazon.ca
Bolton, ON